I'll Fight
for
My Man

Dr. Nakia E. Redmon

MANIFESTED TRUTH * CHILDLIKE TRUTH * TRUE COVENANT FIRM

ISBN: 978-0-578-20513-7

Published by: Manifested Truth Publishing
www.manifestedtruth.org

Printed in the United States of America

DEDICATION

This book is dedicated to all the married folks who have been given both right and wrong advice, have been taught both right and wrong methods, and have witnessed both right and wrong interactions of being married. It's for those who listened and took heed to the advice, methods, and interactions. It's for those who said, "To hell with that. We are doing this our way." And finally, it's for those on the sidelines watching.

CONTENTS

Dr. Nakia Redmon

ACKNOWLEDGMENTS

I want to acknowledge only one person, the one who made this journey possible: my husband. I couldn't have lived this book to write it without him, literally. Despite what anyone believes about life, life is life. You could wish it would have been different, but there comes a time when we have to take the good with the bad and just deal with it. And despite what anyone believes about marriage, marriage is a commitment. I am 50 percent of my marriage, meaning I only can control my half of it. So, along our journey, I've had to learn the hard way to focus on my 50 percent, to make my 50 better, and to smile while I'm doing it. Fake smile or not, just smile. And since my husband is my life, 'til death do us part, and I plan to take the good and the bad, his good and his bad, and ride this thing out until the wheels fall off.

Love you, babe.

PRELUDE

Marriage isn't easy, but shoot, it ought to be amazing, and those of us who are married should be watching out for our marriages—and helping our friends, too. If you ever want to help someone who is married stay married, you must tell them your story. And that is my goal for this book. Under normal circumstances, you wouldn't be confiding in more than one or two trusted friends. But now is not the time to be normal. The divorce rate is on the rise! Time for someone to stand before God's people and speak the truth.

Here is the truth…

1
Someone Lied to Me

Someone lied to me, y'all. And I need to find them and punch them in the face. I'm so serious. And maybe I need to line a whole bunch of folks up and run down the line and slap them. Pow! POW! Pa-POW! I mean slap the taste out of their mouths for being so damn fake. Yes, I said it. Fake! If you want to know why so many people are getting divorced, it's because of the fake married folks around us.

According to the Center of Disease and Control Prevention (CDC) National Center of Health Statistics (2015), for every 1,000 people, the marriage rate is 6.9%. But guess what? For that same population, the divorce rate is 3.2%. So, if I'm reading this correctly, for every two couples that get married, one is getting a divorce. Is it safe to say that we are failing at marriage half the time? I'm sure my simple statistical analysis isn't totally correct, but that divorce rate is still alarming to such a small population.

Correct me if I'm wrong, but according to those numbers, as one couple goes in, half of one has mentally packed their bags. You do know that before you officially leave, mentally you were gone months or even years prior. I will give us some credit; we do hold on, but while holding on, our minds have already left the building. But you see, this is the most critical time. Before your mind clocks out, this is the time to soul search and discover just what has happened in your relationship. And I promise you, I bet you can start with all them folks that lied to you. And maybe even start with yourself. You lied to yourself and guess what? Even while you were officially married but your mind was gone, you lied to someone else.

Let me explain how we all may be failing someone. First, we fail one another through silence. We silently endure the pain. We are too afraid to share what we are going through because we fear the judgment that will come our way. Think about it. People think you are such an amazing couple. And a lot of this may have started before you married. You were a popular person, so guess what? Your marriage had to be popular as well. I think that better explains this point. You as an individual were fake. Never showed the real you all those years. You had plenty of friends, but most, if not all, of them never really got a chance to know the real you. You faked your way through high school and college and now in your own home. So, when issues are brewing, and you really need someone to talk things through to, you are silent. Shhhh, can't share that because they won't think you are perfect anymore. They will start talking about you for sure, and we can't have that, right?

One secret I know is that we are often bound by what we say. Yes, there is power in words. But we are just as bound by the things we never say. I need help. As simple as that. Admitting that you need help. It could be as simple as sharing with another married friend that your husband is starting to disrespect you by calling you out of your name. Or maybe he is staying out longer, and you don't know how to approach the situation. You never know. Maybe your friend has faced this before or has another friend that has. They may have the answer to your issue in their hand, but you will never know while in silence. Yes, I believe that's why the enemy wants to silence our lips because there is deliverance out there, but we never quite get there because we have chosen to remain quiet about our personal storms out of fear of what people may say. Afraid of the gossip. Afraid of the ridicule. Afraid of what our spouse may say if they knew you were discussing "their" business with other people. Afraid of everything you have built unraveling on you all because you opened your mouth. It is at that point you go without healing because you chose to be quiet.

I remember my deliverance during those so NOT magical first two years of my marriage. Go ahead and laugh. And think to yourself: How did your first two years go? Mine were HORRIBLE! Might as well tell the truth and shame the devil, as they say. I'll tell anyone who will listen that I don't know what James and I were doing those first two years! We were fussing and fighting about everything. You think it and I'm sure we had a match about it. Didn't matter what it was. Seems like we just had opposite opinions about anything just for the sake of disagreeing with each other. And I'm just about 99 percent positive you had the same issues with your spouse. Stop me when I get to your street. Toilet paper should be over not under, toothpaste pushed from bottom not the top of the tube, television off not on while sleep, clothes and shoes belong in the hamper or closet NOT everywhere else, bed made daily. Hell, take a shower every day...I mean for real. How did we miss so many differences while dating that all hell breaks loose once you live together? Like day three of marriage, too. Right after your touchdown from your honeymoon, suddenly, we don't know who we have married.

Well, while you continue to laugh at yourself for thinking your marriage was sooo wrong and that everyone else's was so perfect (slap yourself), let me continue on how I was healed the first time. First meaning I've had several iterations of healing along the way. What number am I on now, you wonder. Not sure but the more you are willing to be open, the more opportunities you'll have to heal and live in your marriage another day...month...year. I recall being invited to a girls' slumber party for the young adults at my church. I can't remember everything that was done or talked about, but one thing that stuck with me for years was that I was able to hear other married women share struggles. Then I was able to share that I didn't realize others had been experiencing similar things. You see, during those first two years, I would always hear things like, "Girl, I would've called you, but I didn't want to bother you because I know you all are still honeymooning." Or something like, "Hey there, newlyweds! Still enjoying your honeymoon?" What do you think my response was? "Yep," with a big smile all while rolling my eyes and cursing in my head. Yes, I was rolling my eyes hard because there wasn't any darn honeymoon going on. Shoot, I remember even arguing on the honeymoon!

Once I opened up about my nonexistent honeymooning, it allowed others to share their similar feelings. Hence, we got it all out. Sort of therapeutic if you will. And then after the sharing, some of the ladies with more experience than me in this thing called marriage began to speak on ways to conquer those feelings of thinking I had obviously picked the wrong person to spend the rest of my life with. Apparently, I hadn't made the dumbest mistake. I was experiencing what everyone else was going through yet just didn't know it! I didn't know that it was normal to be at each other's throats at the beginning. It was actually sort of expected because with marriage you did more than just put on new shiny rings. Now, the two of you had to figure out how to live with each other, under one roof, every day for the rest of your life! Forever ever? Yes, forever ever. If this is your "right now." Lift your head and continue to fight your way through this phase. If you have gotten past this, you can now laugh at your current wisdom of knowing better.

Now what do you think is another way we are failing married people? We fail them through the appearance of everything being perfect. And no, I'm not referring to social media pictures of you two smiling. Nothing is wrong with that, and don't let anyone tell you that you are fake when you post or share a cute picture of you and your boo. Here is the thing. When do we take frowning pictures? I need an answer. Talk back to this book. Tell me when you have said in mumbled voice and through gritted teeth, "Turn around, smile, and take this selfie." When has that happened? It has never happened, that's when. We can't tell folks to not post their pictures. I mean that's what some of the social media sites are for, to take and share pictures. The part that makes it fake is when we start bragging through our words about our spouses. "My boo is so caring and sweet. Girl, he spoils me so much, I often can't contain my happiness." Later that night, he is calling you a whore.

"I have the best man. On the weekends, he always likes for us to have date nights without the kids, so we can bond and grow stronger. He is just thoughtful like that." Yes, he has date night with you on Saturday, but what about the evenings after work when he gets off work at 5:00 but barely makes it in by time the 10:00 news comes on without a reason anyone would believe.

If we want to brag or talk about our relationships, we can't tell half the truth. We must be truthful about what is going on or remain quiet. Now, there is a difference in the silence here and the closed lips I just discussed. If you need help, you have to speak up or no one will ever know that you are suffering. And you will continue to suffer in silence, but in this example, it does no good to exaggerate the truth. For me, if James and I are not quite happy with each other, I don't feel required to tell folks. If I have a close friend I can to vent to, I often will tell them just to get it out. But that's not everything or every time. For instance, if I'm upset because he is being messy around the house, I don't always feel the need to share that, but if it's something I'm fuming about and can't quite let go, I may need to just talk to someone about it. It's best to always have a confidant for such things. Someone who can listen and only listen. Someone to answer questions occasionally but overall someone who understands. And it's not a requirement for that confidant to be married, but I'd surely move with caution if they are single. I'm not saying you should throw away your single best friend. They have a role in your life, but it may not be as the keeper of your marriage business. For example, a single person can't possibly tell you ways to respond to your husband from any experience she has. If you think she can, please tell me how. Now that is not to say she doesn't have good advice on how to conduct yourself as a human being, but she or he simply can NOT give you marital advice. Simply put, they have no advice to give from their single seat. Please don't make that mistake.

For me, I had a single friend whom I shared a lot of my strife with, but I chose her wisely. She wasn't just a faraway friend. She was a true friend, and she was, catch this, hundreds of miles away. In a car, it would take me 10 hours or better to get to her. There were lots of benefits of her being away. We could literally talk in secrets. I could share with her without feeling embarrassed. I rarely saw her face to feel ashamed of anything I'd shared. Does that make sense? There was never a time that I had to worry about her and James being in the same room and me remembering something I'd told her. If it were something that pissed her off, they weren't going to be together for her to act funny around him or to give him looks. Surely you get where I'm going with this now. It is often hard to spare feelings when you have upset us over how you treat our friend. That's why it's never a good idea to share your issues or gripes with your family. Family doesn't forgive and move on that quickly, if at all.

Therefore, you need a married friend or two to unload things to. Yes, more than one is all right because if you are true friends, you both will share things that you both don't want to risk getting out to the world. And you can share different things with each of them. Your married friend from college may understand the sex issues you are facing, so when you two share, it is usually about what goes on in the bedroom. Your church married friend may feel you best when it comes to the spiritual issues you are facing with your spouse. They (your spouse) don't or won't pray or attend service as a family ritual, and it bothers you. After venting with that sister-friend, she gives you advice, and she prays for you. The married friend you consider your road dog, y'all do everything together like shop and go to the gym. If you are feeling insecure about your weight and that scoundrel has had the nerve to say something about your baby fat, she just may be the one to discuss with as you two walk the treadmill together. You see, with these individuals, it's most important to be open and honest because guess what? Since you and your friends have opened the door to these discussions, it makes it easy for you all to trust each other with one another's information. They need or will need to unload on you, too, and it's good to share with someone you can trust your deepest darkest feelings with. Marriage has that way of bringing out the darkest things you didn't think you would've imagined feeling and/or doing before. You must not keep it all in. A true confidant is a must in your marriage.

Perception is reality. If what one perceives becomes their truth, how do we prevent appearing perfect? Well for the masses, we can't without professing it, and that's not what I'm saying we should do. You can't go around with a sign or just start sharing bad times on social media. But here is an idea of how you can break that perception. If people think you are the example of what they believe is good and perfect, they will approach you for advice. They will ask for help or make comments about your relationship in comparison to theirs. Yes, some will be bold to make such comparisons, and this would be your chance to impromptu mentor them on the real you. Better yet, it could be your chance to become that confidant your friend needs and for them to become yours. This is not the time to talk about what you think they should do, and it is definitely not the time to talk about what you wouldn't put up with because of how you don't play games.

If you find perfection in another person, and they say something like that to you, immediately stop sharing. I mean stop right there, don't pass GO and collect $100. Change the subject if you have to, but you must realize this is not the friend for such conversations. And please realize that not everyone will fill this role and just be glad you didn't tell them more. Don't be ashamed of whatever you shared. Just change the subject and jump fake back with them. Start saying stuff like, "You know you are right, I don't play games either, and I'll let him know exactly what I'm feeling when he gets home! Girl, did you see that new episode of…" I mean change the subject and move on, honey. This is NOT the one. And next time she comes around and says, "So, how are things?" LIE and say, "AH-MAZING, chile! Glad I listened to you. Have you seen that new show on BET about…?" Yes, ma'am. Just like that. I'm not a person who lies, but if it's between that little white lie about how you feel and telling them the truth that your home feels like hell, tell that lie. No one can check you on your feelings. Some people like how hell feels. Especially when they keep putting themselves in the same situations with the same types of people over and over again. They won't listen to anyone's advice, but when asked, their response is "I wouldn't put up with that if I were you, girl." Therefore, when you realize that's what you're up against, your response should match theirs, and you shouldn't feel no ways about it. "Girl, I love my man. He so caring and so sweet." And move right along.

So, we fail married couples by keeping silent and by trying to reflect a perfect life in our marriage. We hide our own failures or shortcomings. Divorces have become common to us, correct? So, if you have experienced one, it doesn't mean it feels good, it just means you had the non-luxury of that experience. Well, guess who can be the best person for such advice on things not to do? You, my friend. If you tried your best to stay married, and things got beyond your control (and there are numerous reasons why things end in a divorce), and you ended up dissolving the relationship, then you could very well be the person to help save another person's marriage. I'm sure you never really thought of it that way. Every woman for herself is how we have been treating this thing. Misery loves company we say, but there is some truth in that. We are often silent because no one helped us. That person has to figure it out on their own. What a sad thing to think like that. But we do this often, not just in our marriages, but in so many other facets of our lives. We sit by idly and watch the people we call friends...fall. Yes, when we don't say anything, we watch them fall. We know cheating is wrong, yet we laugh with them while they tell their stories of sneaking around. We never utter a word when they brag about disrespecting their spouses with the words they spew out of their mouths. We even help her shop until she drops knowing the house is near foreclosure. We never speak up because we are afraid of losing her. That's right. No one likes to be told they are wrong. That is why people often attack back with YOUR wrongs when you try to help them. And when this happens, there goes the friendship. This is why it's so common to watch them throw their relationship right down the drain.

Maybe this is your second marriage, and you are determined to make it work. Tell me. I'm so for real when I ask these questions because when you talk back to this book, you become self-aware of your feelings and thoughts to yourself as there is no need to lie to me. But tell me, who have you shared your story with? And if you have shared it, were you honest about everything, or did you sprinkle just a little truth here and there, and then hide the rest out of shame? Be honest. I do realize it's hard to reveal the truth, but if a friend is confessing that their spouse is cheating on them, and that is one of the major issues that led to your divorce, wouldn't it behoove you to not sprinkle, but pour out all you can to help that sister get through that terrible time in her life? Yes, but I'm willing to bet, you did not share. If you are reading this but haven't gone through a divorce, but your husband is also guilty of cheating; I'm willing to bet you didn't share this experience with your friend either when they opened up about their new experience with infidelity. And if you did share a story, was it your story to share? Ever notice how some women will share stories of their other acquaintances before you will ever hear a story about them? Yep, if this is you, you are guilty, too. I want to call us ALL out—this includes me.

There have been times when I know I could've

matched my friend's experience with a story of my own, but I didn't. Most of the time, it's not due to a lack of trust, but more so the lack of sharing that friend has done with me. Listen, timeout for telling lies. The reason you are reading this book is the same reason I'm writing it. Marriages are failing, and it's time to tell the truth. We all have played a part, so I can't simply write about what I've heard. I have to speak the truth about myself, too. And the fact that you are reading this is all because so far, if you know me, you know that I'm quite frank, open, and blunt, but guess what? I've failed a few folks, too, simply by not being the first to open up. I have lots of friends and lots of married friends. My husband and I are known for having lots of gatherings at our home. We love to entertain. After moving in to our current home, we actually had a discussion on how it's often hard to stay close to our friends because we are so busy in our own lives. Keeping up with the kids can be taxing on any marriage. And oftentimes, we only congregate with other couples at the kids' birthday parties. Well along the way, we have decided that having birthday parties every year for the kids is overrated; therefore, we chose to stop that "who has the biggest" child party and started getting real about this thing and having more adult parties at our house. We even converted a bedroom in our basement for the kids. When we have house parties, we have two rooms designated for adults in the basement. Usually one room becomes the room for the women folk while the men take the theater room. We eat together and then we go our separate ways to have our girl or guy talk and a room for the kids to have, well, their kid talk.

Now, to be honest, just about all of the couples or non-couples that have frequented our home, most don't really know anything about my marriage. James is a guy, so I'm pretty sure he hasn't opened up to any of them. And I'm the female who loves to talk, and I know I haven't or don't open up to them. Why? Because before now, I've never been brave or bold enough to be the first person to share. Real talk. We hang with each other, we celebrate birthdays together, we attend church with each other, we are even there for one another when one is grieving, but we remain quiet on this one crucial part of our lives. When it comes to our marriage, we are silent. I was silent and am silent with most. Now, should I express my deepest feelings and thoughts to every couple that graces my front door? Well no, but I should be able to share with at least one of them. And before I got on this journey of blogging and opening up more, I honestly was not opening up to any of them about what James and I really had going on. They were only worthy of the happy times, none of the sad ones. Amazing how the enemy has bound our lips together to the point where we don't even share with the people we consider close friends. We trust them with the care of our kids. Hahaha...let me throw it out there. We leave our kids with these folks, yet we can't trust them with a piece of ourselves. Wow. I just slapped some of y'all so hard that my palm reached right back around and slapped my own face. We trust our neighbor with our child but not with our man. Humph, I think I can stop right here because you feel me now. If you didn't agree with none of the first two ways we fail each other, I bet you caught that one.

We have become a society of keeping things to

ourselves until we have no other way around sharing it. I mean, how long can you keep a divorce hidden? Not very long. Eventually, everyone has to know the man has exited the house. Someone will see him move out his things. Someone at church will notice that only you are bringing the kids. You can only hide it so long. The crazy part is that even after the divorce, we still do not reveal what transpired, and if we do, it's only the watered-down version. "Oh, we just couldn't see eye to eye." Or "He needs to grow up." Or "I married the wrong person." One more: "I just choose to be happy single instead of miserable with a man who isn't considerate." Really. Is that the real reason you two divorced? (Shaking my head.) You know better than me that ain't the reason at all. But the way the enemy works, he masters in isolation. He wants to isolate you from your family and friends, so he makes you feel ashamed. That shame feeling will make you dodge everyone you love, even the church. We don't want to answer questions because we know we will lie, so we come up with clichés to describe our problems. Amazing how we will hate a liar but feel forced to lie about who we are and what we are feeling. Want to meet a fake person? Find someone ashamed and there you are. If the enemy can get you in isolation, he has you, and it will be extremely hard to break his grasp. The key is to resist him first and then he will flee.

Before you continue reading this, let me warn you. I'm a very spiritual person. But most importantly, know that I'm a real person. I quote scriptures I've read, but when I do, trust that I've read the whole chapter at least (not necessarily the entire book), and I try to make certain I'm using the scripture correctly from my teachings, my reading, and from my spirit. I will not quote anything I do not believe, nor will I quote something I've heard but haven't laid my eyes on from a personal understanding. I do curse occasionally, but if I curse to express something, I do try not to quote any scripture near those words. You are letting me be real right. Sometimes curse words are the only or best words to express some things. Do I curse often or like a sailor? No, I do not. It is not my second language but more so used sparingly as an accessory in my writing, but I do respect His Word. Will I curse in this book? Honestly, I do not know, but if you see an explicit four-letter word in Chapter 10, but recall reading scripture in Chapter 7, save yourself the judgment and do it now to get it out the way, or denounce me as a spiritual person and call me one of those churching going hypocrites. One thing I am, I am good on anything you can call me. If I'm a hypocrite, so are you. Let me define hypocrite while I'm on this. According to Merriam-Webster, a hypocrite is a person who puts on a false appearance of virtue or religion OR a person who acts in contradiction to his or her stated beliefs or feelings.

Recall, I've boldly stated that we all have helped failed someone with our fakeness or silence. So ummm, yeah, that makes you a hypocrite, too, darling. While at it, I might as well define the word judgment. This is another term we erroneously use way too often in my opinion. Judgment means the ability to make considered decisions or come to sensible conclusions. To judge someone, you are forming opinions or conclusions about someone. Sooooo, how can you determine if you can trust someone without making judgments? Will you be right about that person? Sometimes no, but many times yes. So why is this such a bad thing to do now? To make decisions, any and all decisions, you must judge a person or situation. Yet, the new adage is to scream "Don't judge me." You say this to prevent people from doing something we all do automatically. The issue isn't whether we should or shouldn't judge. The issue is whether that judgment is true. If it is true, sorry, but you have no leg to stand on. Doesn't matter how many people I've wronged in high school, if you my dear, are wrong right now/in the present, it is right for me to come to that conclusion...hence judgment. So now are we good? Judge me as you will. I will continue to tell my truth from my perspective. Who gone check me, boo? LOL. All right.

Now that I got that out the way, just know this about me. I will refer to the Bible for my help with this book. I will also refer to my realness to express this book. Accept it now or close this book and forever hold your peace. One thing is for sure, if you have this book, that means you purchased it, and ummm at this point, you disliking my approach is not harming me. You have the book, dear, so you might has well get your monies' worth and hear what a sistah has to say. See how I just used Ebonics? There will be times I will choose Ebonics over Standard English. Basically, I'm getting all my vices out right here, so you cannot waste time picking at everything you think is wrong with this book. Instead, focus on the message. How dare she use the word 'ain't' in this book! Gone (go on) and get it out now, girl! Get from under your rock of damnation. I do not want to lose you in translation. So much of this book can help you and me, too. And lastly, I do occasionally take commercial breaks like this one here, that has nothing to do with the current chapter or topic. Now, commercial break over.

If the enemy (hence the devil and his army) can get you into isolation, he has you. Think about all the mental trials and convictions you have experienced. Once on the other side, meaning once you have gotten past or beyond the mental jail sentence, have you ever thought about that situation you created? Ever shared it with someone? Most mental issues we have with ourselves are hard to share because we feel no one will understand us and we are too shamed (there that word is again) to share, especially if that person appears to be perfect. We don't like to feel like an outcast, nor do we want to bring that attention to ourselves. Therefore, we keep closed lips about what we are going through, which leads to us not only failing that person who needs to hear that they aren't by themselves on that island, but we also fail ourselves by not allowing us to have the freedom of expression and freedom of deliverance. I don't know about you, but I want to live my life outside of the mental prisons we judge, convict, or throw ourselves into. Step one of this journey is to stop lying to folks.

2
To Fight Means…

I titled this book after one of my first blog posts of marriage realness. Here is where you may get a lot of spiritual/religious type discussions. But don't be afraid of it. Even if you aren't at my level of spirituality, you don't have to be; just keep on living. You may not be religious at all, but if you allow yourself just a window crack of openness to what I am saying, you will be able to recognize and relate to me later on, if not immediately. You know how you squint your eyes when you start to recognize things or when you start to connect concepts to reality (connect the dots)? Well that is what you may experience later on after putting this book down versus high-fiving me now in agreement, and that is perfectly ok. I will take every opportunity to break my thoughts down to the lowest common denominator to make this book plain and relevant to all.

That particular blog post was the scariest to write because I was afraid of what things would come after releasing such an affirmation into the atmosphere. For instance, ever plan a weekend that you just knew was going to be so amazing that you told the world that you couldn't wait for the weekend to come? Well, ever have such weekends to turn out to be the worst weekend of your life? If you haven't, I know this to be true for me. I'd be so excited about something, or I would tell someone of something I was expecting

20

only for things to go terribly wrong. For myself, it seems like the first half of my life was full of such moments to the point I stopped celebrating in advance because I didn't want to experience things not going my way. I started being quiet about my excitement to maybe hear about a job I'd applied to. Now, ask my husband, I express all job interviews to him as if there were mine only to tell him later that I wasn't offered the job. Did this make me stop telling him? No, because one thing I've learned is that rejection is necessary for success. I didn't feel this way growing up of course. But now, I'm wiser and this is a staple in my mentality. I no longer dread being excited about life because guess what, life will happen. But I have to be honest, we often don't mind life happening with some things like not getting a job, but things going on with our households, especially with our husbands, no, ma'am, we don't want to play those games. I wasn't willing to open up that door into my marriage. I didn't want bad things to start happening all of a sudden with my husband. I was very afraid.

But through prayer, He questioned me. "Are you more concerned with what he (the enemy) will do or more concerned with what I can do?" You see, writing for me is more than just throwing words on the page. I often pray over my messages. I pray that what I am saying doesn't offend, meaning I'm saying things incorrectly. Some things will offend people, or better yet convict people when their situation is being called out. Those particular situations I can't help or prevent, nor do I want to. If I publish something that pricks your conscience and leads you to question your own behavior (become self-aware) and/or calls for changes in your life for the better...then good. I do not mind hurting your feelings if it leads to your help. But my goal is never to intentionally speak ill of people in general, which turns them off from reading. I don't do this to keep people reading my material. I do this out of pure care for people. Even if I disagree, I like to spare feelings within the discussion and/or argument. I consider the reader and their feelings; therefore, I pray my message is expressed appropriately, and if He signs off, that's all I need to hit "publish." Trust, those messages I publish without prayer, by just moving out on my own accord, oftentimes, I don't really like them because I later realize I was too much human-driven and less spirit-led.

After realizing the source of my hesitation, I challenged that fear by releasing the message that no matter what, I will fight for my marriage. Hence, I will fight for my man.

Well what does it mean exactly, to fight for your marriage? And why did I choose to gear this toward women? Surely, I'm not saying that women are the only ones in the relationship fighting. Men fight, too. But of course, society predicates that women are often petty by fighting over men. Yet when men fight and/or even kill over women, it is often considered emotionally justified. A double standard at its best. Here, I am out to break down such stereotypical barriers by announcing that I will fight for my man, but it's not in the way the world typically views a fight. That is the beauty of this book of making this fight a good one to have. With the current divorce rate, many don't fight, or they think their yearlong fight was all they could handle, or they decided he wasn't worth the fight based off the lies of those that failed to tell them the truth.

Listen! Let me tell you what this book is NOT. It's not to criticize anyone that has been through a divorce or to condemn anyone currently contemplating divorce. I'm not judging anyone's decision. This book is geared to me and anyone else who is currently fighting for their marriages, and trust, the fight started the moment you said, "I do." It didn't start when you found him late night texting another woman. It didn't start when he didn't come home that one night. It didn't start when he decided to not attend church anymore because of a bunch of hypocrites. Or after you realized you'd married a slob. The fight began as soon as you confessed your life to your spouse. But the sad thing for me and maybe for you, too, is I just realized that I had to fight and go at it constantly.

One thing about me, I've always been goal-oriented, often creating new goals, and my mind on constantly fulfilling them. Ever start a goal only for something to happen to set you off track? You know that was by happenstance, right? Think about the last time you set a goal to better yourself. It doesn't matter what part of your life it was to improve. It could be a weight loss goal, grow your hair goal, go back to school, save money for the down payment for a house, or shoot save money period! Think about the last time you did this and really consider why you got off track. Something happened! Think about the time before that when you were destined to become a "new you." Something happened. If you can't recall, go back to your new year's resolution. Did you even make it to February? What happened? Something. Something always happens to make us decide to put that goal down for now, take care of the issue, and come back to that goal later. But do we come back and pick it back up? Nope. And when we do, it's months or even years later.

Let's say you actually do go back and pick up that goal or better yet, you never put it down. One thing I've learned recently is that when the enemy can't defeat you, he doesn't stop trying or simply go away. If the enemy's direct attacks don't stop you or your progression, he goes after your man.

Commercial break: The enemy is a spirit. It's not an actual person. It can't walk the earth, but to be present, it only needs a host. It needs a carrier. Scripture tells us to resist the enemy, and it will flee from us. Oftentimes, we don't resist, and when we don't, we fall prey to being influenced, used, and/or a carrier of that spirit. We all know people who are carriers of constant evilness. And there are people just like you and I who are influenced occasionally with or without our knowledge of being used. One thing to know, we all are prone to being used. So, it's never recommended to point fingers and criticize those currently being used. Have compassion as your time could be soon. Back to our show.

When the enemy tries to trip you up from reaching the stars, oftentimes, he is successful if he gets to your man. Ladies, it's hard to focus on daily tasks when you are worried about your man. Worried about why he is suddenly upset. Worried about the distance you feel. Worried about the words he just so aggressively expressed to you. Worried if he will come home. Worried if he will answer your call. Worried if his job is secure. Worried if he is being faithful. Worried if he is still on your team! Yes, even in your marriage, the old feelings of insecurity have reeled its ugly head. And when it does, who has time for goals. Forget the gym, you can barely will yourself out of bed. Mainly because you are tired. You were up all night worrying. That's how the enemy works.

The fight is real. If you are one of these new age independent women and married, I am willing to bet many of your goals have become extremely hard to fulfill once you got married. Hence why many of us think it was easier being single. The attacks are hard. They hurt. We don't know what we are doing wrong. It's so constant. Over and over again. Why is this happening? Did you marry the wrong man? Who is this man? What happened to the one you said "I do" to? Where did he go all of a sudden? Where is God now? Has He abandoned you?

NO, He has not! He will not! He will never leave! But one this is for sure, someone else is around and he doesn't want to see you succeed at your goal nor does he want you happy with your man. Marriage is hard! But it has the ability to bring out the very best in you. You can do so much as a team. Ever heard of that? Thugs are very possible individually but put your awesome self with another fantastic human being and you can conquer the world! Yes! So much more you can do when you put two heads together. And imagine how you and this team, your husband can achieve so much and conquer the biggest mountain together far better than you could've ever imagined by yourself. So now, understand why it is important for the enemy to STOP this from happening! He can't let it be so. That joy can't prevail. It has too much power. It can do too much to help so many people. Goals get fulfilled when you have joy! When you and your man are on good terms, you talk and strategize together. You make plans for your family. You set good achievable standards for your kids. You encourage each other and as a team you lift up your kids. Kids flourish in this type of environment. Find some statistics if you don't believe me! Research will reveal that when parents are together on one accord, they have the ability to produce fruit from whence they have planted. Now do you feel me! I'm trying to make this plain. The enemy is out to kill, steal, and destroy! This, in which I type, he can NOT allow it to manifest. It goes against all of his being. He must stop you. He must prevent you from reaching the stars.

And when he gets done with you...what star? You will have completely forgotten all about that goal that you had set for yourself. You sat it down and forgot because you have more pressing things to do. You have to fix or rebuild your home. It's hard to go home to a man you have lost touch with. Forget a goal! Your goal is to make it to the next morning. It's hard to lay beside someone who you think doesn't think you are beautiful anymore. What? He is in the guest room. And you think you can devote time to a dream when your current dream is sleeping in another room. So yes, trust I know many of you are fighting right now. And it hurts. This is the worst fight of your life. You can't spend time on getting back to you when you have this kind of stress looming in the air. This is the fight I'm preparing you for.

How do you currently fight? Are you fighting with your words? Screaming obscenities at him? Throwing up his past ways in his face? Bad mouthing his family? Attacking his character? Does that make you feel better when you do that? No, it doesn't, and you are making it far worse. You are not helping the situation at all.

This is the fight I want to prepare you for. Now that you are aware of the tactics of the enemy, the focus should be on two things. One, recognizing the presence of the enemy sooner rather than later. Now that I know some of his ways, my battle is far different than when I simple chump things up to having a worthless man. The quicker I realize the hand that I've been dealt, the sooner I can play my card (the highest spade) and stop the turmoil from existing in my home instead of festering. So, first is knowing the root of your problem and second, know how to properly fight against it.

3
Let's Get Ready to Rumble

For me, I think the honeymoon lasted for about one month at best. Maybe two. I say two because I do recall being out of town for a training class for three weeks, the week after we returned for our honeymoon. So that month doesn't count, but I won't make my marriage sound like a horror movie, so let's agree to one quarter, so three months. It took about three months before my face started to frown at the clothes. Yes, clothes. Clothes may not be your issue, but clothes were certainly mine. You see, my husband loved to dress in the latest fashions, especially with his shoes. And he had expensive taste, rightfully so. I married a bougie man. Not like myself, he never had to want for much that he wasn't adorned with. There was that huge difference between us, but ironically, it never was an issue for us. It was just our thing that was different but never discussed or relevant.

My husband literally grew up in a big brick house on a hill (not a cliché either). He grew up with both his parents and sister. So, this was my imaginative family. Not that I envied their family dynamics or anything, just coveted the house. My dream as a child was to grow up and earn enough money to have a nice big house. This could've been every child's dream. There's something exciting about a house with large rooms for your toys and space to host your many relatives when they come.

My upbringing wasn't as lavish as his, but it was decent. I lived with both parents as well. My father, at home, was my step-father technically, but he treated me like his daughter. He had been around since I was a toddler, so no one knew or remembered anything different. Just like my husband, I had a sister as well, and ironically, we both are nine years apart from our sisters. No big house on the hill. We didn't stay in one location the majority of my childhood. For elementary, we lived in the south side of Jackson, MS, then west side for middle school and then back south for high school mostly. For my senior year, we went back west. So, I didn't have childhood friends like my husband did. I can't speak for him, but my family had some rough times in there that I'd wished were better, from a child's perspective that is. I'm sure the things I wished I had more of, like more clothes and toys, James had. And I do know he had mostly name-brand things from his mom's account. Such things weren't afforded to me, but I was brought up well nonetheless.

Well some of this will play out in our household later. That's why I decided to give a CliffsNotes account of our upbringings. His being a little more privileged on the wealthy scale while mine was a little more humbled and on the less lavish scale. Even though my husband came up with more, with different taste, his behavior toward me and my family never reflected that. It's like it didn't matter or went unnoticed. He would come home to Jackson with me and stay in modest quarters with no issue. My family home had a shared bathroom with the master bedroom being the only room with its own private bath. However, my husband grew up with every bedroom with a private bath. He never let on that visiting ever made him uncomfortable, and I appreciate that about him.

When did the fighting start for us? Well, since we are being honest, the fighting began in the engagement period. Yes, it sure did. Think back to that time and be honest with yourself. Just like me, you really didn't think you would make it back then either. Listen, I love my husband, but I started doubting us while we were engaged, shoot before engagement. Didn't I say my husband was bougie? He didn't just have bougie taste. Hell, his attitude was bougie, too. I couldn't tell him nothing because in his eyes, he could do no wrong. You're probably thinking, "Well, why did you choose him?" It's simple...because he chose me. Dating is hard. One thing I had promised myself was that (while dating) the next guy I get serious with has to be more into me than I am into him. Reason being, and you know this, us women, we love hard. And as we love hard, we hurt harder. When I put my whole foot into the relationships, I had been hurt every time, and I was so over it! No longer would I continue to allow someone to damage me in this way, so I decided that I wouldn't put a toe in until he exposed two of his first. James did that for me. That's the piece that made me cling to him because he had a way of expressing his admiration for me that I cherished. I can recall prior to us agreeing to be boyfriend and girlfriend (hmmm, I wonder if they still do this today), I was taking a three-week training course in Syracuse, NY. This was doing the time when we were on the phone all night talking about everything and then listened to each other's breathing for the next one or two hours. Do you remember that? Wasn't that like the best feeling ever? Goodness, I'm getting chills thinking about how that felt just so good to the soul.

James made a comment about traveling up there to see me. He was living in Texas at that time, and my home was Alabama where he was born. I'll spare you the whole story, but God has a way of putting two people together. I know James was meant for me! Well, I agreed that he should come visit. I assumed he was just talking. Next thing I know, he was booking a flight and on his way that very weekend. You see, he was infamous for doing such things, making me feel special. No doubt in my mind—he was infatuated with me, and when he was happy, I was happy. But the challenge was when he wasn't happy and getting past his often-bad attitude when he wasn't getting his way. You see, my humble upbringing was never a concern for him, but with his spoiled background, what was important was for him to get his way about things. When he felt he was getting the short end of the stick, this often caused him to shut down and essentially, he would shut me out. Imagine coupling that attitude with one of bluntness and independence. His attitude and my mouth equal a bad combination.

Once the fighting started (not physical), it seemed like it would never end. I mean we fought about everything. You name it, it went down in our house about it. Now mind you, I'm writing this, so it's all from my perspective. You will get none of his side in this book. He will have to write his own book if he wants to share his side. This is ALL about me, so let me tell it. Dude took up an entire guest bedroom with his clothes and shoes. I mean he treated that room like it was a closet. Ladies, if you and I have anything in common, that room was supposed to look and be guest-ready at all times! I don't care if we haven't had a single guest all year. When one walks past that room, it should be immaculate, in my opinion. You can imagine how this aggravated me to the nth degree. And I couldn't say nothing to him about it. Whenever I did, we fought. After a while, you get tired of fighting and saying the same thing over and over again. I'm sure he was tired of hearing it as well, but he was stubborn about it and would continue just to spite me.

In addition to his clothes, I had expectations of what this man was supposed to be doing around our home. He should be taking out the trash, keeping the yard cut, bushes trimmed nicely, cars washed and maintained, home repairs taken care of, garage neat, pick up after himself, pay bills, and help me with anything I couldn't get to if I asked. Honey, let me ask James to wash the dishes. First of all, when he did, he would use enough dishwashing liquid to clean the dirt off of the desert. Besides paying bills, the rest of that stuff was done whenever he felt like it. Now, I'm not saying they didn't get done at all, and we lived in a pigsty. He did them but on his timing. Hell, I wanted them all done on my timing, every Saturday. Like wasn't Saturday the cleanup day for everyone? That is the way I did it growing up, so it had to continue in my household. That's just the way things go, right?

Wrong. Now don't frown your face at me. You probably had those same expectations. You just didn't realize the error of your ways as I didn't.

In hindsight, I know my expectations were wrong

to place onto him, but you couldn't tell me that eight years ago. In the midst of our mini battles, you couldn't have told me I was the one causing most of our issues through my own lenses. We will discuss that later. For just another moment, let me keep on venting! James loved to dress up, but at home, he was relaxed—too relaxed. Couldn't he had found something other than those gray jogging pants? I mean he wore them every day when he got home and on the weekends, clean or not. I remember for Christmas buying him several pairs so he could switch them out at least. But I guess it was something about those gray ones because he continued to wear them. I'm sure I said something to him like "You don't have another pair of jogging pants you can put on?" Like I was serious. It was a turnoff that's for sure.

Let's not even discuss sex. I didn't want it! Well let me say it better than that. It's not that I didn't find him attractive. It just seemed like we weren't reading each other right. For instance, I didn't know how often or what he wanted. I'm sure any man spying at this book would think I'm crazy because I should've just assumed he wanted it all the time. He probably did, but I didn't know how to approach him. Crazy how once you say, "I do," it seems like rules suddenly appear out of nowhere. New laws and bylaws. A revised constitution of some sort. We just got uncomfortable with each other for no darn reason. Somehow things were different, and I'm not sure either one of us knew why. But one thing is for sure, we didn't know how to express it. Didn't know how to start the discussion or what to say. So, we just continued as if we knew what we were doing.

Sex was rehearsed most of the time. How often? I

can't recall, but it became a source of our arguments. He said I wasn't aggressive, meaning I didn't initiate our escapades. Yet, I thought I was. I'm the one who came on to you on Saturday! I'm the one that told you to meet me in the bedroom that other time! How can you say I'm not initiating sex!? And don't come at me talking about it's not enough! Or we haven't had sex in a long time. I swear he would act like seven days from the last time equated to him enduring seven years of famine. It was ridiculous. Hell, if I'm being honest, it's still ridiculous. This part has never changed. Fast forwarding to the present, James still acts like going a week is prison time. But so much has changed from then until now, so off that break and back to the past.

I want my readers to understand that our first two years weren't our best by far, but it didn't stop us, and I'm glad I continued. I believe those first years are meant to be crucial because when you think about it, two people are trying to merge their lives together. Both James and I weren't fresh out of college going into this relationship. We were finished with school and somewhat established in our careers. I had even purchased my first starter home. James was living in Texas at the time we started dating. As interns with the U.S. Army, we met in Texarkana, TX, working at Red River Army Depot. As part of our job requirements, interns started at that location but would then move to other army installations. James got selected to remain there while I moved to Huntsville, AL. Just so happens, James was born and raised in Huntsville, and his parents and sister were still there. Look how God works.

After James and I started dating, we discussed his

moving back home so we made a goal timeframe for him to return, and he actually arrived one month prior to that goal. Later that year, he proposed. I was extremely excited but scared at the same time. You see, James did love me, that I knew, but recall I said he had a bougie attitude that would eventually be the foundation of our stumbling blocks. His attitude plus mine, yes, we were in for a treat. So yes, I was excited this man asked me to be his wife, but I did have my doubts; I can't lie and say I wasn't worried. Again, why agree to marry him? Well, number 1, he was infatuated with me, and number 2, he had a strong family foundation I adored. I knew in my heart he would take care of me and our future family. I didn't have to worry about him running off or anything. Sure, there are no guarantees in life, but I truly believed this in my soul. And that was rare, in my opinion, so no way I was going to let a real good man get out of my grab. I'll take his bougie ass attitude, and we would figure it out. If that's all he had against him, I'd take that. Hands down.

Our engagement period was a period of our life that had assumed a title, but overall it was still a little on the flowery side of things. That was the period one would assume you could use to iron out any wrinkles you may have found along the way. Get issues and problems out of the way before you walk down that aisle. Puuuu, it sure was not. During that time, issues were small and insignificant. Nothing big. We were that happy and excited about getting married, but we hadn't done anything truly to get us prepared for what was really in store for us. We thought we were ready. Everyone said we were. We were such a cute couple they said. James so funny. We would be great together, they said. From the outside looking in, I can see how they came to that conclusion. We both were careerists wanting for nothing. No kids. Just air and opportunities.

All was good in our world. I was planning the wedding of my dreams and working on my doctorate degree. I loved a challenge, and that degree was one of my long-term goals. Time was definitely not being still. And I'm such a different person that I can't truly describe it, but I had a show planned for my wedding where I would perform/dance during our reception. Me and two of my girls would dance to a hit song at that time by Beyoncé called "Single Ladies," and we did another dance with a compilation of other hits and oldies. As I planned the wedding and worked on school assignments as well as worked full-time, there was no other time to deal with things outside of my set routine. James came over often and spent the night sometimes. Wedding was vastly approaching. Maybe two more weeks to go. Everything was going well, so I thought, until I got on my computer at home and realized James had left his email account up and open. Hmmmm, what did you think I would do? Of course, I would be nosey. Hell, so would you.

An old adage says, "Go looking for something and ye shall find it." I can't say I was actually on the hunt for something. It sort of just fell in my lap. Well I stumbled upon messages from two females that I didn't know. One he apparently associated with at work and another one, well umm he didn't really know her. He had or was in the process of hiring her for his bachelor party. Why was he the one booking her? You are asking the wrong person. I don't know how those things operate, but that is what he told me back then. His conversation with the "lady" from work as he referred to her wasn't all that bad. She was mostly complaining about her situation at home, but what caught my attention was a message where she asked him for help paying her cell phone bill I believe it was. I'm not saying I liked knowing someone was comfortable enough to ask my fiancé for money. Reading it did bother me, and I'd get the story on this, but what I'm saying is that it wasn't as harmful as the messages I would see between him and miss stripper. Sounded like galloping horses in my chest as my heart raced while I read the messages between them. It wasn't a lot. Doesn't matter. The fact that she was excited to see him was enough for me to consider this wedding that was happening in a couple weeks. Well, surely, I couldn't call it off. Or could I? Should I? It was time to talk to James and get to the bottom of this.

How naive I was. Of course, I took his word for it. The 'lady' was just someone he'd met at work, and they both would confide in one another. Her about her problems at home, and he would talk through issues of ours with her. You know how you remember where you were when 911 occurred or when Kennedy got shot (if you were old enough during that time) because those events are so sketched in your brains that you can even recall up feelings from that time? Well, I can remember walking around toward the front yard of my house, cell phone to my ear, explaining to James that when/if he has a problem with me, he was to take it to another guy friend if he couldn't bring it to me. He was to never be discussing our issues with another woman/lady or whatever she was. I then checked him and said, "She is your friend...she isn't a lady." I wasn't crazy. Later on, I would learn more about this lady, whatever, his friend girl. Oh, and I didn't forget about miss stripper. I had to look him in his face on this one, so I didn't reveal I'd read those messages until he came over that evening.

In hindsight, I'm sure he was lying. In exasperation, his arms flopped up and down as if he was about to fly away as he explained it was nothing just guy talk (locker room banter as it is often referred to). He swore he didn't know her besides through those messages and that he wouldn't dare touch her. I assumed other than their regular stripper booking interactions for his party. Either way, this was something I had to pray on because it didn't sit well with me—just as your face is frowned now reading about it. He said he wouldn't have done anything, but had I not caught it in advance? Ummm, yeah right. I'm sure I blocked it. Whatever it was to be.

After praying for a sign, asking God, "Should we be getting married?" I did hear for myself that it was ok to proceed. I can't lie though; I was so scared to ask God because I knew He'd answer. I just wasn't sure of what His answer would be and how I would handle it had He said no. But since I had His blessing to continue, we continued on with our plans to get married, and oh boy, did we have a wonderful wedding day. My day couldn't have gone more perfectly. Everything was elegant, gorgeous, and so much fun. We had a really good time, but as we all know, with everything that had been done prior to our big day, none of it prepared us for what was in store next as husband and wife. Weddings are all cute and so overrated, but the real fun happens in the days to follow.

4
What I Learned about Nagging

My vow in writing this book is to help others, so please remember that. Therefore, I will not sit and just rat out my husband without telling my part. I now know I played a role. All those things I vented in the previous chapter about, how do you think I handled revealing to James that I didn't like those things? Well to him, he'd call it nagging. He was right to an extent. Of course, I deemed the mentioning was necessary. He needed to know if he was doing something to upset me, so I had no choice but to express it, right? Well sort of. Nothing was completely wrong with me sharing my dislikes with him, but how was my approach?

Let's face it. There is never a good time to express these things, so you might as well let it out. When it came to his clothes in the guest bedroom, I think I approached him with a little agitation in my voice, frown in my brows, and pointing. "Can you put that stuff up in that room?" Of course, it didn't stop there.

That's too easy. "No reason for all that stuff to be on that bed. That room needs to be cleaned. There are plenty of drawers and closet space." Are you imagining the look on his face? I'm sure you got his words down. "You always got something to say about something," James would say, meeting my level of aggravation. Now here came the fight.

To me, he needed to hear that, so I didn't know why he was upset. I refused to clean up behind him. At the time, we had no kids, so there was no reason for me to be cleaning behind a grown tail man. Originally, I tried to be the good wife, whatever that means. I would cook often, fix his lunch on occasions, wash and fold his clothes, and essentially kept the entire house up to par. I'm sure he doesn't even recall me ever washing and folding his clothes because that trip didn't last long at all. Maybe a weekend turnaround trip because after a couple of times finding his drawers all amuck, I just refused to re-fold and re-fold and re-fold the clean clothes for his drawers to be neat. Plus, why would you mess up all my hard work? But really did it for me was to find worn wife-beaters thrown back in with the clean clothes. When I realized he'd worn that shirt and put it back into the drawer, I was DONE. D.O.N.E. Done. Stick a fork in me. I QUIT!

So, our routine was starting to set in. He'd do something, and I'd make a comment, then we'd fuss, argue, and/or fight about it. No physical fighting, but loud talking was just as bad at times. Or he wouldn't do something, I'd comment, fuss, argue, and fight. Or he'd forget something, and I'd comment, then fuss, argue, and fight. I mean it was ridiculous. One thing about my husband, he holds grudges. I don't. I'm the one who gets over stuff way too fast. So, I'm over it, and he is still fuming or not saying anything at all. And he would wear his feelings on his shoulders. So, if we were out and about after a fight or in close proximity to one another, he wouldn't say two words to me. Sometimes, depending on where we were, he wouldn't speak to anyone else either. So, guess what? I'd have to tell him about that, too. No way was I going to let him treat me like that in public, especially not around my friends. I recall telling him, "If you have a problem with me, have it with me at the house. No reason for you to be out with your face screwed up. You need to fix your face. I don't do you like that."

Have you ever heard that men tend to go into a cave when they have issues? It's their way of coping and thinking, and sometimes it leads to them coming out with decisions being made. I think I've heard them being referred to as 'cave experiences.' Well my husband was infamous for his cave experiences. It took little or no effort on anyone's part to entice him to want to go into this mental cave. I think he even vacationed there. I'm making light of those experiences, but they were very disturbing at the beginning as I didn't know how to handle them. I didn't know what was going on and often attributed them to something I'd caused. My inadequacies as a wife, or unattractiveness from the pregnancy weight gain, or my inability to be glamorous all the time, and the infamous lack of sex. That last one for sure. Everything seemed to stem around sex. The longest we'd go without it was 5-7 days, and he would always elude to it being like it was months. NEVER had it been over two weeks. I mean give me a break. Maybe it felt like that to him, but trust, as woman, I was keeping track in my head. Maybe not so much tracking back then because we were so not traditional about it. Or whatever that means.

It didn't take much for him to desert me for that cave, so of course, me nagging about the little things was just another reason for him to pack an overnight bag and head for what was becoming his favorite place. Ladies, I know some of you remember having a little overnight bag you reached for or even kept in the trunk of your car for those random, wished for nights you'd be over too late and he'd ask you to spend the night instead of driving back home. Well imagine that is the type of bag my husband often had laying on the floor on his side of the room. As soon as I'd ask about the shoes splayed over the floor, imagine him not only picking them up but as he grabbed them, he'd grab that bag and head for his cave. He'd enter, turn the lights on, and put out a sign that read Do Not Disturb.

I'm pretty sure this is how we spent our first couple of years. I'd say something and off he went. It became our new normal. But of course, this was not how things appeared from the outside looking in. Oftentimes, people would make comments to us on how perfect of a couple we were. All we could do was smile and laugh but not agree. But we could say, "Noooooo, we aren't perfect. We have problems just like everyone else." And that wouldn't be far from the truth at all. Matter of fact, it was all true. But of course, in our eyes, we figured everyone else had it going on and that we were the only ones at our stage of the marriage with such problems. If we only knew what was really going down in others' homes, we wouldn't be so quick to misjudge our own efforts. That was one reason why I felt the need to author this book. Too often, we are looking upon others and becoming envious of what they have. Wishing our marriages were as good as our friend's marriages. Everyone else appears so happy. Just not fair, I know.

In addition to all of the clothes and shoes everywhere, it seemed like we were clashing over just about anything to do with the house. I recall noticing how quickly we were running out of dishwashing liquid. I only noticed because prior to him moving in, dishwashing liquid would last me for months. But now it was running low way too fast. One day I realized what was going on after coming in and seeing him prepare to wash the dishes. And before you frown at me because you are wondering why I would complain about him washing dishes; he didn't always wash the dishes. Trust, we had to fight about that too. We agreed when he moved in that he would handle everything outside and I'd take care of the inside. None of which I had an issue with, but the problem came in because he wasn't taking care of the outside during the 4-5 months that required yard work. He probably cut the yard once every other 2-3 weeks, and he'd do the front yard one week and backyard the next and trimming hedges was not an option. After I caught on to his routine or lack thereof, I made it known that I desired help around the house. He disagreed of course, but once I explained that it wasn't fair for him to only take care of the outside during the summer months and have no responsibilities the rest of the year; he eventually started pitching in. Now that he was washing dishes, I just so happened to walk past him preparing the water and pouring I know what seemed like half a cup of dishwashing liquid into the sink.

I didn't say anything the first couple of times I'd noticed the mound of dishwashing liquid going into the water that produced enough soap suds to reach the roof. You'd be proud of me. I know I was. But after two weeks had passed since the last time I'd purchased dishwashing liquid, and it was time to buy more, I couldn't help myself. I didn't want to argue, so I had to think about the words I'd say to James. Told myself to say it nicely and that is what I thought I did. I approached him while he was in the kitchen getting ready to prepare the water. Picture this. I said, "Babe, I think you are using too much dishwashing liquid." He said, "What?" I repeated what I said, and that was all she wrote.

James went off on me. He told me it made no sense for me always having something to say about everything he did. He was washing dishes because I complained that he wasn't doing nothing, and then I had the audacity to have something to say about using too much dishwashing liquid. I felt terrible. And I silently cried as I replayed him yelling his feelings and thoughts to me. He even wanted to know what the tears were for. I sadly explained that I was only making a comment, and he questioned why I even felt the need to say anything at all. That made me feel worse. It was just dishwashing liquid, but did I not say "babe?" I didn't say it mean at all. I thought I was putting sugar on the top as I spoke the words, so how did it turn around on me the way that it did?

Well, sometime later, I realized James had had enough of me. It didn't matter how I was saying it. Didn't matter if I said "baby, pumpkin, dear heart, sweetie pie" when I stated what I did. It didn't matter how small or insignificant the statement I was even making. James was so used to hearing me nag about things he was doing or not doing, that eventually it all sounded like a nag. It didn't matter if I was trying to come onto him, if I opened my mouth to utter sweet nothings in his ear, it would come off as a nag. That was how bad it got between us and the things I just had to say or tell him. Wasn't that what we were taught? I recall being taught that if I let him get away with stuff that he'd never stop doing those things, and it would be my fault for letting it go on for so long. I couldn't let him get away with treating me any kind of way, right? If I did, he'd never respect me. So, I had to let him know the error or his ways or end up living with a man bossing me around and walking all over me, right? So, I had a reason for telling him each time I felt he was out of line. I just had to. I couldn't help it. It was what I'd been taught to do. So, what was I doing wrong?

Instead of getting closer together and enjoying our life as newlyweds, we were fighting like crazy. Either I was messing it up with nagging, or he was complaining about our sex life. One week we didn't do it enough, or I wasn't aggressive enough. He swore he had to always be the one initiating sex. But that means we were having sex, so how can you say it isn't enough? I couldn't win for losing. Less than two years in our marriage and he was already tired of being the one that 'had' to be the one initiating sex. I'm sorry, but if YOU are the one that wanted it, hell then it seemed about right that you'd be the one passing the love tap first.

I may be by myself here, but I've never been the

one for sex. I'm still not the one always wanting sex. Doesn't mean I don't like sex or like it with him. It can be fantastic, and I still not want another round the next day. I can't explain it. It's exhausting physically and mentally. Wears me out. I enjoy it, and it still feels good to go days without it. I said days. This man of mine doesn't go weeks without it and nor was this the case back then. So, I didn't understand his complaint back then, nor will I understand it now.

I decided before we end up in a bad place, let me try to shut up more and add more sex into the marriage. Maybe that was a bigger issue than I realized. I tried to be more aggressive. But it wasn't enough. I'd rub on him as my way of letting him know that we could have sex, but he wouldn't take over. Ok, so let me try something else. Maybe that wasn't aggressive enough. Maybe a message would work. One evening I surprised him with a note. Nothing long. Just a simple note of meeting me in our bedroom. That song by Silk came to my mind. You'd think this muscular figure would be in our doorway, but no one stood there. Instead I got a text back saying, "If you want it, you come get it." What wait. How was my advancement becoming an issue? "You said I don't initiate sex, so I sent a message saying I wanted you to come here," I sent back. An argument was brewing. He responded, "So if you want it, you should come in here and get it." I can't. This shit was becoming too petty. I'm going to sleep, I thought, and that was what I did. Screw him. Well, not really because no screwing was going on. I would not do this back and forth. Wouldn't be arguing that night. I'd try again another day, I guess, maybe.

One day he was in the shower in the hall bathroom, and I had just gotten out of the shower in our bathroom. After drying off, I walked over to where he was and knocked on the door. He opened and looked at me. I don't recall what he said, but it wasn't much as he closed the door. I stood there hurt. Crushed. Did he just turn me down? Yes, he did. I stood there with my ass out, and the tears started to flow down my face as if I was still in the shower. My heart was in pain. I can't explain this feeling, but it was like a burning sensation in my chest like none I'd ever felt. I tried to compose myself as I walked through our bedroom back into the bathroom to get dressed behind a closed and locked door. But before I got dressed, I had to get the loud ugly tears out. They were muffled by the towel I held over my mouth and an extra barrier as I sat in our closet on the floor getting that release out. I'd never experienced such rejection before in my life. I wasn't sure how to take it or what to do next. More heavy tears escaped. I was literally butt naked, and he closed the door on me. He turned me down. Who does that? He did. He did that to me. ME! It was clear now. No way I was mistaking this. My husband didn't want me.

5
What's Done in the Dark

Never mind everything that was going on with us. We continued trying to act married. We faked our way through our first year. I kept myself busy with work and school. I was a fairly new supervisor, and that was stress in and of itself. A young manager at that. At age 30, and I was managing some people who were my parents' age. Oh, what fun. Young manager and young wife. I'm not sure which was the hardest. Probably the latter. Each position came with many references I can refer to (i.e., books, training, gossip, etc.), but neither trumped the actual experience one had to endure as the real teacher. I was successful at work for those that were watching me. You could say the same for my home life; however, I wasn't feeling that way. Needless to say, I did like most newlyweds, I introduced a baby into the equation. We didn't quite have ourselves together, and I'd gone and gotten pregnant.

James was extremely excited. For some reason, he

yearned to be a father. For a man, he actually envied our other married friends that had kids already. He wasn't pressuring me or anything. It was just the way he acted around them. He always held the new babies and gave them a lot of attention, and of course, this was noticed by those around us. People would always make comments while smiling at him along with questions for me like, "What are you waiting on?" or "You don't want kids?" or "When do you all plan to start trying for kids?" All the questions folks thought they just ought to ask you—it's like they couldn't help it. "Oh, you are married now, so when are you going to have kids?" as if being married wasn't hard enough. "One day" would be my response, and I'd leave it at that.

Maybe this would help our relationship. I'm sure we all have thought this when having issues within our marriages. The kids will help us to grow closer together, right? Well, for a little while, I will agree. He was the most helpful during my pregnancy. He would go out of his way to make sure I was comfortable. He would brag to his friends and anyone that would listen. It didn't help that I was expecting a boy. Having little boys just does something to a man's soul. Whatever that something is was happening to my husband. He was proud and so was I. Maybe he did still love me. We would make it now. I was carrying his baby. No way he would do anything wrong to the one carrying his seed.

We celebrated our first year of marriage, and I was just four months pregnant. We went to the beach, and he took great pride in telling every waiter that I would NOT be ordering any beverages. I'm laughing just thinking about this. They'd say, "Can I offer you something to drink?" James would immediately respond, saying something like, "Yes, some tea for her because she can't have any alcohol," with a frown that quickly turned to a smile. Then he'd rub my belly and announce that I was expecting.

I wasn't even that huge, and he still felt like he had to protect my whole body. He was very sweet indeed. Coming to all of my doctor appointments. Joking around with my doctor and the nurses. Who would've imagined us starting off so rocky? He was acting like a daddy with mommy. All the way up until I had to have an emergency cesarean section. After the doctor announced he couldn't wait any longer and that he had to get the baby out, James asked if he could have a second alone with me. The doctor said no. While they prepped me, James prayed over me. That was one gesture I'd never forget. We were going to be ok.

James Henry Redmon III was the light of our life. He literally gave us life. Daddy James kicked into motion. I decided to breastfeed my son, and it was not quite like how the book explained it to me. It wasn't going well at all. Trey stopped latching on to my left breast, but I was determined not to give up. I couldn't give up. Other mothers breastfed until their kids were one and two years of age. Surely, I could handle this. I kept trying, but nothing was helping. It hurt like hell. Eventually, I decided to give up my left breast and just allow him to feed off of the right one. This was possible. Think about those women who had twins. Well, I acted like I had twins, and with that, Trey would be the right breast twin. Whatever worked. But the thing was, it wasn't working either. I had to start supplementing with formula.

I recall one day sitting on my bench bed holding

Trey up against my breast and crying hysterically. I couldn't figure out what I was doing wrong. He wanted to eat every hour during the night and whenever I gave him formula and tried to pump, nothing was coming out. He was only two weeks old. Where was my milk going so fast? I might as well give up, I thought, as I choked off of my tears. James walked past our bedroom, but he didn't know what to do, so he just left me with my rain shower. He couldn't take my tears, but I knew he felt he had to do something. The next morning, I woke up late. Wait! How is that possible? I had a baby that needed to be fed. Well, Daddy James took it upon himself to close our bedroom door and care for his son while Mommy slept in. He gave Trey the formula we had to hold him over until I woke up. Boy, that was the best sleep in the world. I felt grateful to have him around. So thankful that when it was time for him to return to work, I didn't want him to leave me. And he didn't. He stayed with me another week longer, and I was one happy camper.

Trey was 4 months when we experienced the scariest event of mother nature. The tornado of April 11, 2011, entered the home of my in-laws as we camped out in their underground shelter. The wind got into the house and slammed the shelter's door. After the door slammed, everything got black and quiet. I'd never been in an actual tornado before, and I will never forget how I felt on that day and the days to come when news of thunderstorms were heading our way. The simple thought of rain was producing anxieties within me. I started following our meteorologist on Facebook so I was in constant knowledge of weather patterns and predictions. My heart would pound uncontrollably as it rained. No sleep for the weary as I had to stay watch until the rain subsided. I recall one night going into the closet, getting on my knees, and praying for our safety, for my mind to be at ease, and for my heart to slow down. That tornado left me emotionally scarred, but nothing like the next tornado that was to come to our home.

Trey was about 6 months now, and things were just going okay. We were on and off again, depending on the day of the week. We wouldn't argue around our son, but we would often send a lot of nasty emails to each other throughout the day at work. There is a saying: what is done in the dark shall come to light. I'll lean more on the latter here because I've never been one to go looking for things. I believe if I'm supposed to know about it, I will know. It will be made plain, and that is exactly how this incident went down from beginning to end. It was time for such things to be revealed.

This particular weekend, something wasn't quite right. James had an attitude with me, and this time, it wasn't my fault. I for real hadn't done anything. He just started acting funny with me for no reason. If I asked a question, no matter how simple, I'd get a smart remark. After asking over and over again what was wrong, he'd harshly express he was fine and then just ignore anything else I had to say after that. Something wasn't right here. This wasn't his normal behavior, and I knew for a fact I'd done nothing. So, what was it? Funny how I recall up a scene from one of the Madea movies. I believe it was the actual play (remember Tyler Perry did plays before he produced the movies) Why Did I Get Married? Remember that one scene where the daddy was talking with his son after his son yelled at his wife and made her run off crying and upset? He questioned his son's behavior by asking, "What did she do?" The son started talking about his wife aggravating him, and the father said, "No, not your wife but that woman out in them streets." The father shared that for him (the son) to come home fussing and carrying on the way that he was, it wasn't that anyone in the house did anything, it was that he was upset with his other woman.

Such thoughts took over my mind because I knew I hadn't done anything, and his attitude was at an all-time high. It was now Saturday night, and I remember walking from our guest bedroom toward our bedroom. To the left, I could see him sitting in our love seat in front of the TV. He was looking down at his phone intently with a slight frown on his face. Something in me stirred. I realized by time I reached my bedroom, which was less than 10 feet away, that something was going on with him, and it was on that phone. What he was doing was on that phone. But I was not that kind of girl. I didn't go snooping into someone's phone. I was better than that. I wouldn't let him lower my standards. I'd never been the insecure time, and I wouldn't start now. But my answer was on that phone.

The next morning, like always, Trey and I went to my church while James attended his. Yes, we attended separate churches. This wasn't my idea, and I didn't like it, but it was the hand I was dealt. Before we started dating, I'd always prayed for a man that loved the Lord enough to not love Him from a distance but to attend church on a regular basis. Well, that part of my prayer was answered, but I never imagined needing to be more specific like which denomination. Who would've known that was something to even ask about. So yes, my husband was a churchgoer, but his denomination was one I would never accept as my own with good reason. Judge me all you want. Yes, I prayed for a man I could worship with but denounced his church.

After the man of that church brought me in to tell me that I wasn't saved all due to the denomination of my church, no way would I allow my son to grow up thinking millions of Baptist worshippers, such as his mom, was going to hell due to the 'type' of church one chose to attend. I can understand if I didn't believe in the Lord, or if I never went to church, but I was a Christian who worked daily to remain on the narrow road and do things that Christ would approve of (not man). To be approached like that and learn how many of that religion felt that way and taught those things, no ma'am. I was a believer in the Lord as my savior. I believed in the Trinity. No house would question my relationship with Him, so yes, outside of petty arguments, we had this one huge elephant sitting in our living room every Sunday morning. And that elephant wasn't moving.

As long as I didn't visit, everything seemed to be ok. But the issue with that was, if I didn't occasionally visit his church, I would definitely get a NO when I wanted him to visit mine. But to prevent that humongous argument, it was best I didn't go because I'd always have something to say afterwards. I just couldn't help myself. To help with this, I made this the top of my prayer list that 'my family will worship together' one day. One day, I heard the from the Lord on this matter. It came from two ministers (ironically, women ministers) I didn't really know from a personal perspective at my church. It was the pastor's anniversary, and Pastor Rance Allen from The Rance Allen gospel music group was visiting, so of course, I had to attend both services that day. I was approached during prayer by one of those ministers who told me in a nutshell that God heard me and that He said to leave it alone because He was working it out. After that day, my main goal was to SHUT UP. I would not make another comment about our church situation. I would trust in the Lord to work our situation out, knowing my family would worship as a family in one church, and we would be happy.

That promise would soon be tested. It didn't take years, and not too many months, before I would have to recall what those ministers told me that day. It never fails. Each time you on the verge of a breakthrough or just given hope of one, the enemy is on the prowl. I'll go into this more later because you will need to know how to handle such times. Trust, it took me awhile to recognize these patterns and to figure out how to handle them. At this time, all I had was to *shhhhhhh*. That's it. I must remain quiet! This for a person who had to say everything *now*.

James had taken up bowling on Sunday evening with this league, so it was his normal to be gone on these evenings while my norm had been to cook a big Sunday dinner and to prepare for the work week. I'd gone inside of the guest bedroom, which he was using as his closet, to put something away and noticed his iPod on the bed. My suspicions went back to the night before on how he had been acting mean all weekend. Like I said, it was not like me to look for anything, but something told me to look through this device. But how? It is password protected. Believe me or not, I picked it up and entered in the first thing to come to my mind and just like that, it opened. Wow. It actually worked. I was in.

I scrolled through the apps. Nothing really stood out. The most common places I suspected to check would be text messages and emails. His messages weren't linked to this device, so the next best thing was to check his email messages. I opened the mail icon. There weren't a lot of messages on there, but that email greeting didn't look familiar. It didn't say hey James Redmon, and it wasn't his Yahoo account that I was accustomed to. It was a GMail account, and that username I knew nothing of. He had another email account. MF.

Even though I knew nothing about this account, apparently, two other females had free access to it because the email addresses were definitely names of girls. They had open access to my husband on here. They had his attention here. I couldn't believe what my eyes were looking at after opening the first message. It was a picture. I tilted my head to the side a little in confusion as I knew those weren't my lips on here. Are you serious! I go to the sent box to see what he had to say about this. "I like it" is what I read. Really. You like another woman's private part. I reply back to her. Think I didn't? You're a fool. Let me let her know how disrespectful this is. And let me tell his behind as well.

"SO YOU HAVE PICTURES OF ANOTHER WOMAN'S PUSSY, HUH?" I spoke venomously into the phone after he picked up.

Of course, he had to catch his words as he

stuttered, "What are you talking about?"

"That email you have from some girl!" I explained.

Stuttering more, he lied, "That's why I told her to not send me stuff like that anymore!"

"Stop motherfucking lying! You told her you liked it."

"I, I, I, ok, I shouldn't have. I'm sorry."

Putting an end to this, I said, "You not sorry. You a lying motherfucker. You got a whole email account for your women. You on there talking and liking pictures from this chick and oh that 'lady' you used to talk about to me. Funny how she has access to you on there, too, but not me. FUCK you, James!" I hung up. He kept calling, but I didn't have any more words for his lying behind.

He wouldn't be home for a couple more hours, so I went to re-read and re-read those messages. There weren't many, but I read them all while my stomach ached and heart pounded. I couldn't tell what was going on between the "therapy" lady. For the most part, she was complaining about her husband still. I was still livid because he had more back and forth with her than I'd gotten from him lately. Go figures. He liked talking to her obviously and this other chick, well, I would have to investigate more.

I searched both of their names on Facebook. The picture girl looked to be a little older. She wasn't bad looking, I'd give her that. She had older kids. Oh really, she was from the town he moved from when we were engaged. So, she wasn't here. This was a good thing, but still, it didn't excuse his behind at all. Didn't matter if she were overseas, I would not tolerate such disrespect. What if I had a penis pic within my email? He'd have a 10-pound baby out of his! After going through her pictures, I drew my own conclusions of their relationship. Regardless, I had more questions, but not right then. I had to see about this therapist. She was on Facebook as well, and I'd seen her name before. She had commented on a couple of the pictures James had posted of the both of us. She wasn't really cute at all, so if anything, he probably had something romantic going with the picture chick, but I was sure he hadn't touched the therapist one.

He arrived home, and his mood was solemn. You could tell he was walking on eggshells. He was quiet and so was I. I didn't have any words for him. I just kept replaying things in my head. I was even thinking overall about our marriage. I couldn't put my finger on it, but something wasn't quite right with us. It hadn't been for a while. This weekend had shown me this. My instincts told me something bad was going on, and I stumbled upon this email account that he hid from me. And now my instincts were steady talking to me, saying the same thing over and over again. This wasn't it. There was more. But what could it be? I'd checked that email account and actually got to his Yahoo account, too, but nothing was there. That was obvious. He was being slick by keeping the dirt on that secretive account. I was still hurt by that, too. I kept reminding myself that my husband created an entire email account for them. Not me but for them. There was more. I just knew it.

When he got home, he was silent and so was I. I had nothing to say to him. All I knew was this motherfucker wasn't getting in my bed. Since his clothes were kept in the guest bedroom, he had no reason to come in our bedroom. No reason to knock on this now closed and locked door. I hear him moving around the house, trying to be quiet. Usually, he was a night owl, but he went to bed early this night. The house was quiet. My mind wandered still. I was still pissed. I couldn't believe him. While I sat in bed, all I could think about was how he was going to wish he'd never done this to me.

It was time to go back to work. Goodness, it would be the longest Monday in history. It was so hard to operate at work with such baggage on the brain. I knew my focus would be off as I could barely get out the house that morning. My spirit was just vexed. If you've ever felt like this before, it's like that feeling you get when you just KNOW something isn't right, and your brain is running 100 mph, and it won't rest. Not even for a second will it slow down to let you do the simplest things like finding something to wear for the day. I'd been standing in the closet for way too long just staring at the clothes. I needed to hurry because I had to get my son ready to be dropped off at my in-laws' house. James dropped him off in the mornings, and I picked him up in the evenings, which was great because it gave me a moment to visit with my road dog. For some, this is a little hard to believe, but my mother-in-law means so much more to me than just my husband's mother. She and I hung out together, shopped together, and loved on my son together. That's why dropping Trey off in the morning was not an option. I'd never make it to work on time. LOL.

Usually, James left the house before I did. Just the same now. He was a guy, and I had so much more to do to get ready in the morning. But not this morning. I couldn't quite sleep, so I was up a little earlier and didn't feel up to putting much into myself, so I just threw on comfortable clothes that didn't need ironing. Basic makeup face was all I could stomach. Just a little powder and eyeliner. Forget foundation, eye shadow, and blush. Flat shoes would do as well. I didn't have much to give; I was sorry for those who had to look at my red eyes and solemn expressions. I tried to smile when it mattered, but for the most part, I would just remain at my desk and hope no one needed me.

We exited the house together, but as he passed me, something came over me. I stared at him as he passed by and noticed his work BlackBerry phone in his hand. My heart thumped rapidly as I got in my car and let the window down. He stopped by my door. I put my hands out of my window and requested his BlackBerry. He had a confused look on his face as he handed it to me. I knew it had a password protecting me from activating it. I motioned for him to take the phone. "Unlock it," I stated softly. He started to protest, but I interrupted, "You are up to something, UNLOCK IT NOW!" I demanded through gritted teeth.

After he handed it to me, unlocked, I rolled up the window and started scrolling through the phone. He'd kept this phone pretty clean. There were less than a hundred emails within all the different folders. Any of the calls came from the arsenal, so nothing was alarming from them. We both work on Redstone Arsenal, a Department of Defense Army installation. The arsenal is huge! He and I worked down the street from one another. Probably less than a quarter of a mile from each other. But there are so many buildings and many miles within the arsenal's footprint.

Hundreds of organizations are housed there. It's like a little town within a town. One could get lost out there easily. But another thing to note is that since it's an army installation, entry in and out of buildings is often restricted. Meaning you can't just walk into any building without being greeted by security, and if you don't have someone there to escort you around and be ultimately responsible for you during you visit, you will not be allowed in.

Before backing out of the garage, I rolled down the window and handed him back his phone. He asked, "What are you looking for, Nakia? There is nothing there. Nothing else to find, I promise."

"Yeah right," I muttered. I rolled my eyes and backed out of the garage, leaving him there standing with his palms facing upward as if I was supposed to feel bad for requesting his phone. No, I did not. Like I said, there was more to this story. I was not stupid anymore.

With light traffic, it normally took us about 30 minutes to reach our respective offices from home. This ride was a blur. My heart was still racing and my mind still thinking at the same pace. I made it to work but didn't get out of the car. Sat there thinking. Something was going on, and I had to find out what it was. But I had looked through his iPod thoroughly and didn't see anything else. I checked his BlackBerry. As my eyes squinted, I realized what I was looking for was on his work computer. My body began to heat up as I pondered on it. We both worked nine hours a day. He and I emailed more than we actually talked on the phone. I figured if he and I emailed each other, and he had that other email account for when he was at home, then chances were positive that he was emailing them or someone while he was at work. He had plenty of opportunity to cheat at work. I passed my building and headed heading straight to his location less than a mile down the road from me. My fingers began to tremble as I dialed his work number.

"I'm outside. Come let me in," I nervously belched out.

"Outside of where?" he asked.

"I'm outside of your building. Come let me in," I stated with a little more confidence.

He began to stutter a little as he questioned my intention. "Wha. Why are you outside? I mean you can come in. I'm just wondering what is going on."

This wasn't like me. I occasionally visited, and it was normally after he'd invited me over for lunch or a holiday gathering.

Forcefully, I stated, "You are up to something, and it's there in your office. So, come outside and let me in now so I can get to the bottom of this!" He started to mumble something, but I added in a little more fire: "NOW!"

6
Divorce While Holding the Baby

He arrived at the main side entrance of his building, and I watched him exit and head toward me in the parking lot. I could've gotten out, but I didn't move in order to give myself a moment to calm my shaking hands and the rhythm of my heart. My heart felt like it was about to explode out of my chest. Oh God, what am I about to uncover? Are you sure, Lord? I didn't know how we got here. Nor did I know how I decided to come to his job to search for something. I mean what exactly was I looking for? But I didn't think of this. This wasn't me. I'd always prided myself on not being THAT girl. The girl who doesn't trust her man. The one who always questions his whereabouts accusingly. The one who always picks a fight with her man when he makes plans with his boys. Always nagging when it comes to his freedom. I knew I nagged, but this was the one thing I didn't nag about. I gave him free range to be with his friends as long as I knew where he was, he came in at a decent time that is conducive to the activity he is engaged in, and he respected our marriage while he was out. Watching a 7 p.m. football game with his buddies shouldn't cause him to come in at 3 a.m. Bowling with his league he enjoyed so much should never have him out past midnight. None of these acts had he committed so what was I after exactly?

I didn't know. I really didn't know. I didn't know why I was at his job. Once inside, what would I do? Like why was I here? My heart, ouch, it hurt, and I couldn't stop it from beating so hard. I couldn't. I couldn't breathe!

He was almost at the car. *Girl, get yourself together*, I thought. *You've prayed to be revealed whatever is going on, and the whispers in your ear led you here, so man up and get out of the car.* I didn't hesitate either. Got out and started walking hard, switching toward his building as if I worked there. He was walking as if he was the visitor. An onlooker wouldn't know if we were together or not because of how focused on the door I was. No talking or looks or gestures toward one another. I was on a mission, and I only needed him for access to what I was after. Whatever that was.

Once at the door, anyone watching now would know James was checking me into his building. I had to have an escort in his building. This wasn't the case where I worked. Stuff like this made it hard to just show up on a brother, but I think I'd crossed that. I couldn't sneak up on him, but I surely could demand my way in for such a time as this. After handing over my license and entering my information on the sign-in sheet (name, office I was visiting, organization I was from, clearance, time in and out), I was ready to get this over with.

His office wasn't far from the entrance, so we were there in a few seconds. They had a strange setup over in this building. Where I work, the managers' offices are in the center of the floor and outside of them are the cubicle farms. Here, they had mini offices that housed about four cubicles for the many teams to work together in. Even though it was four cubes in this small space, James had a lot of privacy. Not that I was worried about anyone seeing me or not. I didn't plan to even speak. No time for chit chat. Hoped I was not considered rude, and I didn't care one way or another at the moment.

Luckily, the girl up front wasn't there, and the older man to the left didn't notice I'd come flying through the door like a non-intruder. I could hear the guy who sat to the right of James, but if quiet, he wouldn't know I was here. I was actually hoping I could get in and get out unnoticed.

I sat on James' chair and looked around for the computer button. Forget looking. "Turn the computer on," I demanded in a low and controlled voice. I was surprised at how calm I'd gotten. I was no longer nervous with a heart feeling like it was protruding out of my neck. James turned on the computer, and I waited until it powered up. *Geesh, hurry up. Why does it have to run so slow the day I'm here? Come on! Come on! Come on!* I felt like I was robbing the bank, and the cashier was taking too long to fill that bag up. *Hurrrrryyy up*, I yelled to myself or to the computer, or to whoever was listening.

The computer loaded up, and it looked like any other computer, so I was comfortable with driving and taking it from here. I opened his Outlook for his emails. Geesh mother of Jesus! He had a gazillion folders credited. How did I know where to search? I glanced through the emails in his inbox, but those were the ones I could see from his Blackberry, so that was not what I needed to be wasting time looking. A message was coming up, and I almost ignored it, but then James was acting like he had to handle that message for me. What I needed was for him to move out of my way and give me the mouse back. Then, suddenly, he hit the delete key, and something began to delete.

"What are you doing? Why did you do that?" I asked angrily.

"Nothing. No reason." Nervously, he explained, "Something is wrong with my computer. I always have to call help desk when it does that. It does that at times."

But I didn't need him trying to slick delete nothing from me. "Move. Give me the mouse back. That can wait!" I said.

He sat back down behind me in his guest chair. Here came his neighbor talking over the wall. I heard him stand. Shit, he knew we were there now.

"James, you know...oh hello there," the neighbor said.

Hurriedly, I said, "Hey," and then I turned to face him with a smirk. "How have you been?"

"I'm fine," the neighbor said before turning to James. "I was just about to tell you about this email, James, because I knew I heard you, but didn't realize you had company."

His voice began to sound muffled to me as I swung around in the chair to go back to what I was doing as if it was normal for me to be there. He was still behind me as I was looking at the many folders not knowing and thinking about what to do next. There were so many. *Ok, just read the titles.* I read a few while James fake-laughed and talked with his neighbor. *Hmmmm, archives.* My eyes land on that folder, but nothing could be in that but old emails. Why would he keep old evidence of wrong discussions? Shoot, I didn't think I would, but that was the only title that didn't look like engineering or other work-related jargon. *Just take a look, it won't hurt.*

"Oh ok, it was good seeing you," I thought I heard the neighbor say. That was my cue to act fake, too. "Ok, good seeing you. Have a good day!" I half-turned to tell him.

Now back to business. *Archive folder it is.* Well there were some messages there, and it looked like they had the same subject. As I scrolled down some, the subject changed. *Ok, so the subjects aren't bad, but why keep so many messages of the same subject from a co-worker. A co-worker...maybe.*

I took a chance and selected one. MOE. Read a few lines. Oh, this was indeed a personal conversation, and yes, she worked out here somewhere. So yes, it was a she. But I couldn't read through all of this back and forth. And yes again, they were going back and forth. A sentence here and there between them, but definitely an all-day type of correspondence. I knew I couldn't waste time reading, so I double-clicked on the oldest message of the same subject to open it up, hit send, and then began to enter in my email address.

"What are you doing?" I heard the shaky voice ask.

I ain't scared. "I don't have time to read this, so I sent it to myself. Looks like you were having a good conversation with that *lady*." And yes, for a third time. There was a lot of back and forth between him and that "lady from work" that he used to tell about me. Unh huh. The same lady who was having problems with her husband. The one who asked him for money for that phone bill. Might as well see what they were talking about.

"Funny how you and this lady seem to talk a lot. I knew she was more than you were letting on. She is your friend I see," I said, venom spewing out of my fangs.

Next subject, SEND. Next. Next. Wait. Subject changed, and there was a new girl. Same rhythm here as well so I continued my beat. As I hit send on this one, I asked, "So who is…"

He began to stutter, so I turned to look him in his face. He tried repeatedly to gain his composure. "Who is she?" I repeated through my teeth with eyes squinted.

"Ju-just a girl I was talking to?" He finally got out.

"Just a girl, huh? Talking to her about what? She just another lady you talk about me to? Huh!"

"She is a girl I know. And we were talking about stuff we shouldn't have been talking about. But that's it! Nothing ever happened!"

Livid, I turned back to the computer. SEND again and again on another message and again until suddenly James was under the desk. Wait. Hold up. He snatched the cord out of the surge protector and just like that the computer was off. Screen black.

I couldn't believe he just did that. "Where are your keys?" I stated firmly as my body got really warm suddenly. He held the keys up, and I grabbed them. Took the house key off. Mumbled enough for him to hear me as I walked off, "Find a place to stay!" And just like that, I was at the guard station before my next exhale. He was beside me because he had no choice, I had to have an escort to be walking around this building. Handed my escort badge, wrote the time down beside my arrival time, and kept my head lowered as I waited impatiently for them to return my license. After they handed it to me, I was out quickly. And yet again, we were appearing as separate parties just so exiting this place at the same time.

As I got closer to my car, James lobbied for my attention, but I ignored him as best I could because I was afraid I'd start blabbering out curse words in the open parking lot. And who needed that sort of attention on their job? He grabbed my arms, but I pulled back instantly to be released.

"Keep your hands off of me," I did manage to get out.

"But wait, Nakia! Let's talk. Please."

"Did you sleep with them?" I didn't hesitate to ask. But he just looked exhausted with his hands moving all which of ways. So, I asked again as this was the only thing I wanted to talk about.

"Did. You. Sleep. With. Them?"

He finally admitted, "Yes. Yes. But with just one of them, and that's it. It was just one time." Sounded like all the air was just let out of a tire as he spoke that last part. The expression on his face was one I'd never seen before. So sad. Weary. And it was screaming apologies in 10 different languages. I almost wanted to hold him and comfort him as I sucked in the pain from his face and his body language. But I didn't. I reminded myself of what he just said, and I spewed out, "Lie! That's a lie. It was more than one time." And with that, I was back in my car preparing to leave.

He pulled on the locked door as I put my car in reverse. As he stood there looking bruised, I couldn't look his way. I turned the car in the opposite direction of him, and I focused my vision straight ahead. I tried so very hard to hold the tears, but it was so not working. Why did I have to be such a wuss? I didn't want to cry. I had to go to work, and as a supervisor, there was no way I could simply ignore my employees all day.

My building was just down the road, so I didn't have to go far. That meant it was not enough time to have a good cry and fix my face nor time to allow my red eyes to return to their normal white color. I made it to my building in a blur. Didn't even remember the two traffics lights I drove through. I believed I was driving the speed limit at least. I needed to pay attention because as we arrived to work, people were moving in and out of the cars in the parking lot, and I didn't want to hit anyone.

"Focus for just a moment, Nakia," I told myself, but it was so hard. Those damn tears were starting. I just wanted to go into this building and make it to my desk. If I could just make it to my desk without seeing anyone, I probably could make it through the day dodging people. Oh goodness, several folks I knew were walking in the parking lot. I slammed on the break when a woman appeared from between those cars. *Focus, focus, focus.*

Well, well. Who would've imagined me finding a parking spot near the front? Someone was exiting their spot as I made it to row two. See, the atmosphere was on my side. Maybe that meant I could make it through the work day. Make it through the work day from what? Oh, and just like that, those thoughts escaped me as I celebrated this parking spot. But they quickly flooded back in. Oh yeah, that. My husband was cheating on me. How convenient! I mean we had only been married almost two years. Actually, our second anniversary was coming up soon like in a month. How sweet. We didn't even make it to our second anniversary without this SHIT! Now I was pissed!

"Done sat here and had this man's baby! Baby is just 6 months old. Oh, but he wanted kids SO damn bad. I mean he was jealous of every friend we had who had kids. Always coveting their kids as if they were his. All in their face looking at me like when would I have some. And I give him a son and that was not enough!" All of these raging thoughts were in my head, and I knew I couldn't go in there. It was too late. The fury had arrived, and I couldn't stop the raging waters. Just go home. Just go home and hide yourself for a few days. But how? I was a manager. I couldn't do what the employees did. I had to be present and accounted for. What would they think of me? Well my boss, a man, would understand. Not that he would understand how I was feeling. But he would understand the situation I was in because he was a man, and this was the kind of stuff men were prone to do. Right? Wasn't this what we learned as girls? Our man will cheat? So why was I crying? This was expected to happen, right? But we hadn't even been married two years. And I had this man's child. The one he silently begged for. He didn't want me for real. He couldn't have and then went and did this. He used me. I was for show. Smart, cute, with a good job...no, a high position, too. He got something good when he got me. Yet but how? He cheated. He cheated after I had this baby. He didn't love me. Happy anniversary to me.

As all these thoughts invaded my headspace, I picked up the phone and decided to pull up my big girl panties and call my supervisor. On the first ring, he picked up. *No time to change my mind and hang up. So just get it out.* "Hey. I won't be able to make it today," I said with a shaky voice.

He spoke to me as if I was his daughter with an exaggerated whisper, "Hey now. What is wrong?" With more control, he asked, "Are you ok? Are you hurt?"

I couldn't really say anything because I felt I would just let loose on this phone. I could hear him stand slowly from his seat. Maybe to pace around. My boss was a true man. A fixer! "Where are you right now?"

"I'm in the parking lot," I get out.

"Where at in the parking lot? I'm on my way out," he expressed as if he was grabbing his tool belt, hammer, and saw.

Next thing you know, I found myself feeling like a lost child waiting on my parent to locate me in the middle of the mall. He and I met toward the front of the parking lot, but a little out of sight of workers arriving. He had a grim look on his face as if he'd betrayed me. As he walked up, he tried to catch my eyes, but I couldn't look at him. He had always been a conscientious man and knew how to handle all his women employees without making them feel uncomfortable by invading their space.

Firmly, he asked, "Are you ok? Are you hurt?"

Glancing up, I replied, "No, sir, I'm fine. Not fine, but I'll be ok."

"Tell me. What's going on?" he asked firmly yet

gently.

"I just need some time. I don't think I can function today," I explained.

"Now you know you can take all the time you need, but I need to know if everything is truly ok. You called, and I can tell you were upset and you have me worried."

For a man I've often teased on not knowing how to handle personal conflicts in the office, I must admit I felt vulnerable, yet I trusted him in that moment.

So, I confessed, "I just found out my husband has been cheating." I kept my head held low, periodically looking around to see if we had any guests eavesdropping. No one was within distance.

"Aw now, girlfriend, I am so sorry!" he stated as he slightly moved in, disappointment. He usually talked casually, using descriptors as "girlfriend" to express being on our level as our pal. This time it was less funny but took on the resemblance of one of my gal pals saying it. I mean he was doing a really good job. One day I will have to thank him for making me feel comfortable. Before now I wouldn't have ever imagined having such a conversation with a dude, especially not with my boss whom I've often had to coach on how to handle the women we worked with. And now look at him, doing a great job helping me to keep my composure.

"How do you know that to be true?" he asked.

"I got this feeling that something was going on. I saw some disturbing stuff on his phone over the weekend. This led to me check his work phone, but I got a feeling something was on his work computer. I went to his office and got onto his computer and found all these messages. He confessed." I still glanced around, not really looking up at him.

The man revealed himself now. "You did what?" I just nodded. "Nooo. Now you can't be doing that!"

"I can, and I did."

Even though he wanted to emotionally be here for me, he was still a man; therefore, his body language looked as if it secretly sided\ with James right now. If he and James were friends, I was convinced for a split second that my boss would leave me and go call James to encourage him versus me. Man code stuff just got in the way here, but he corrected himself real quick. With hands out trying to regain his composure from the shock and disbelief of what I'd done, he said, "Ok ok, now that that is done, what are you going to do?" Then he laughed slightly and said, "I just can't believe you did that. You are one brave little lady. I mean done went to the man's job! All right! All right! All right!" He moved his long arms in a flapping motion. He went on to say, "All jokes aside, baby girl, do you need my help with anything? Just let me know how I can help you. What are you about to do right now?"

I looked away from him and around and then to the ground. He had lightened my load, but I didn't want to start back crying. My simple response was, "I don't know. I took the house keys from him. He can't come back right now, but I don't know. Right now, I'm about to go upstairs and get those emails. I sent a bunch of them to my email address because I couldn't read them. So, I plan to read and see what was going on and just go from there I guess. I don't know. Just hurts right now. I don't know," I finished saying and eventually looked up like "Well, and that is that."

We gave each other this sort of "Well, that is that" sort of nod, and I told him, "I need to get something out of my car and then I'll be up. Should be ok to come back to work tomorrow, but I will definitely keep you posted. Just need a day to wrap my mind around all of this."

He interrupted and said, "Look now. You take all the time you need. Just keep me abreast of how you are doing, and we will take care of this stuff. Don't you worry about it."

I really appreciated him in that moment, and so I said, "Thank you" quickly as I felt the tears coming and turned around and walked off to my car. I needed to grab my purse but thought it best to check my face and dry these current tears off and gain my composure before I walked in. I stared at myself for a minute, but I had to turn away from my own bloodshot eyes and red cheeks. It was obvious I'd been crying as I was only missing the puffy eyes, which were promising to come later. I needed those messages, so I reluctantly got out the car, leaving my purse behind, with the goal of going upstairs to my floor and making a dash in and out without being noticed.

Purse hugged tight to my body as some kind of support, I walked through the parking lot avoiding the sidewalks where others might be. Once I got to the door, there were a couple people waiting to get onto the elevator, and of course, I didn't have it in me to have small talk, and it wasn't like me to ignore people, so I decided to pass them and take the three flights of stairs to my floor.

By the time I made it up the stairs, my nervous emotional wreck self was extremely exhausted. Geesh, one would think I didn't work out, and I usually complete 3-4 days of cardio a week. But right now, my heart felt like it was about to leap out of my chest through my mouth. I couldn't walk around huffing and puffing, so I had to get control of my breathing, I forced my mouth shut so the air could move through my nose as my chest rose high, then low.

I quietly reached my desk, trying not to disturb my neighbor. He was slightly deaf in one ear, so if I set my purse down and sat quietly, he wouldn't know I was there. I moved around like a mouse because I didn't want to risk the chance of him coming over. If he did, he would ask what was wrong, and it would be loud for everyone to hear. With him not being able to hear out of one ear, he talked very loud, and that was not what I needed that morning. I sat over in a corner window spot. For my division, we were only allotted two offices for the three supervisors. I'd only been a manager for about a year, and the two offices were occupied already, so I got the luxury of this corner desk, which I loved because it was off to the side, away from everyone who worked for me besides this one guy. But the downside was that I didn't have a door in which I could close for privacy. Had that been the case, I would've came into work today, closed the door, and pretended to not be in for as long as I could. That would've given me time to settle down some. Maybe. I didn't know.

Softly, I typed my password into my computer.

Once I had the computer up and running, I opened my Outlook mail and waited for all those messages from my husband to come in. Fourteen of them finally arrived. I opened one and started to read it, but it was rather long, and I still didn't want to risk someone coming over. I began forwarding these to my AKO (Army Knowledge Online) email account because I'd have access to these emails at home. Although I forwarded the emails, I was still curious, so I scrolled all the way down on this first message I opened to read. I had a 30-minute drive back home. Too long of a drive to not at least read one email.

And here it was. The one whom he was talking inappropriate with. I see now. They were planning to meet somewhere. Nashville. Wow. She was married with kids. They were planning to meet out of town where she was supposed to be for work. "Well, let me go to the latest message from that subject to see if she agrees to meet up with him." My curiosity had the best of me, so I opened each message within that trail to get the full story. They were talking about me. What did I do? Oh, I'm not aggressive enough, he said. She was agreeing with him and understood because her husband was boring, too. Oh really, I thought. He went on to tell her that it was the same positions over and over, and he always was the one who had to initiate it. And he was tired of it.

I hurt more as I read this. He was tired of me. Tired of always being the one to come on to the other. How could he be? The few times that I did come onto him, he didn't get hard. So, hell, I thought it was best to wait on him to get ready and make that uncomfortable setting easy for the both of us. One second pissed to the next second sadness. *Well, maybe he wasn't ready because he doesn't like me anymore. My husband doesn't like me anymore. He prefers this BITCH*, I screamed in my head.

My mind wanted me to close out the message, shut the computer down, and get out of there. I couldn't continue to read those messages and keep my composure. But then it dawned me on. This chick worked out here. I decided to see if she was on Facebook. You know Facebook is the modern day Yellow Pages. You can find anyone on it, along with a picture of not only them but their entire family depending on their privacy settings.

And there she was. This one was pretty. Not like the first one. The "lady" at his job wasn't cute at all.

Commercial break: And before you all start looking around the office, they didn't work together long. They were only in the office together for a few weeks. So stop trying to be nosy. I see you. Looking around, trying to figure out who the work wife was. Hahahahaaa, and trust, I'm not giving out identifiers of any of these women. I'm not THAT woman. I don't want to ruin their marriages as they attempted to ruin mine. So, let's carry on with the story. Break over.

I was not a hater. This new chick was pretty. I was not offended with that at all. My offense was with James and the things he was telling her about me. See that was how mess got started. They could relate to one another. They weren't happy in their marriages and found solace in sharing their miserable marriage stories with each other. That was what brought them together and allowed them to form this *relationship*. Some of you will not call this cheating, it was just two people talking. Whatever, this is cheating. He had feelings for her, even if it wasn't much. What's important to identify here was the fact that he definitely wanted to do more with her. The writing was on the wall. He wanted to hit it.

Now recall she worked on the arsenal, this huge

government installation with over 10,000 employees housed in 100 buildings or so. Redstone Arsenal runs the length of the city. Anyone new to the arsenal could attest that one would need to use their Maps app on their phone to find directions to get from building to building. I could recall many years ago when I started here—my first week of work, I had a printout of MapQuest directions that stayed in the car until I could remember my way. And I didn't go far off of that path. It would be years before I would see other areas miles away and be comfortable with exploring this land.

With that, it meant she could be anywhere out here. So many tenants and organizations were housed within the many buildings. From this one message, I read where he was going to her building after work to see her. His last message stated that she should look for a red Tahoe. In that timeframe, the next message from his BlackBerry told her that he was outside. Here it was. My man going to see another woman. I was sure he was dressed nicely. He had always been a fly dresser. So, I imagined him stepping down from his truck and straightening his pants leg over his Johnston & Murphy's. I wonder if he hugged her or if they stood there uncomfortably. My blood began to boil as I pictured him asking if she wanted to sit in his truck in my seat and possibly going over and opening the door for her. After stepping up, she'd have to shift a little here and there and straighten out her clothes while he walked around to his side to hop back in. Still a little uncomfortable, he'd adjust the radio and maybe ask something he had already asked her earlier that day like "So, what are your plans for later? How long do you have before you have to head home? Do you have to pick up your kids or him?"

I literally held a visual of their entire interaction within my head as if I were on the back seat. Goodness, to be a fly on the back seat, one could only wish. I shook myself from my trance as I typed her name into the address lookup option within our Outlook. There she was, well her name rather. Her last name was a very common one, but I wanted to see if she mentioned whom she was married to on her Facebook account. I searched through her pictures and found a family photo. He wasn't tagged, so I didn't think he had a Facebook account. To the comments, I went. Often, someone will say something like "Awwww look at you and John. Y'all are so cute together." Dead giveaways are often left as crumbs on a person's page. You can literally determine a person's entire life and family tree from Facebook.

There! A name. I decided I'd go back, but first, I wanted to see if I could find another picture or something to verify that that was his name. I kept hitting an error indicating there were more pictures. Now I was in a zone. Whether I saw his name or not didn't matter as I tried to figure out the life of this woman my husband had gotten involved with. Picture after picture. I was at a point that I had forgotten what my goal was. Like what was the purpose of what I was doing now? Oh yeah, needed to determine buddy's name. Since I'd somehow forgotten, I went back to previous photos because I might had actually seen him and forgot to stop to read the comments. Now I was going back through those profile pictures. Nothing more there that identified mister. To her albums I went next as there was a strong possibility one might be called 'family.' How naive we are. All of our business is usually on the Book.

I did eventually find a picture that confirmed her husband's identity. So back to the address book and yep, he was there. I should write him. I double clicked on his name, making it appear in a new message. I typed in the subject line *Your wife and my husband*, but then I backspaced that out. What about a simple "hey"? No, he might think it's spam. Then I tried "Information about your wife." Backspace. Delete.

I had to be mature about this. He hadn't done anything to me. So why would I email him? No need in doing that. My issue was with James. I *did* have slight beef with her because they were discussing me. She was asking him questions about me. She knew about me and still told him it was all right for him to just swing by her building. I did understand very well that she didn't owe me anything.

I then corrected myself. She owed me nothing. But I bet I would let her know that I knew about them. Now that I could do and nothing was wrong with that. I went back to the address book, this time double clicking on her name. Subject line was easy this time. I typed *YOU WON!* This is what I wrote her:

Hi. This is Nakia, and apparently you have been talking to my husband, James. No worries. I have no plans of being nasty or mean. Just wanted to let you know that it's funny that there was a time when I thought I only had to worry about the single hoes wanting what belongs to me. How foolish of me. Didn't know I had to worry about the married ones, too.

Is your husband's name, ######? I wonder how he

would feel if he knew what you and my husband have been up to. Like I said, no worries. I have no plans on telling him and ruining your marriage as you have chosen to ruin mine.

YOU WON! He is all yours.

I reread my note to her to make sure all words were spelled correctly. I didn't want to sound ratchet with incomplete sentences and misspelled words. After everything was ok, I hit SEND. I made sure all of the other messages were sent to my AKO account so I could finish reading those at home, logged off of my computer, packed up silently, slowly picked up my keys and purse, and headed to the elevator.

Once I safely made it out the front door, I could lift my head. As I walked to the elevator, I had looked to the floor with a slight ease up on my face, trying not to make eye contact. But now that I was outside, I naturally let my eyebrows go back to conversing with one another. If you know me, you know I suffer from RBF. Resting Bitch Face. A frown is constantly on my face even when I'm thinking happy thoughts. All throughout school, people would ask, "What's wrong" and I'd always have to explain that nothing was wrong and that my face just looked like that. It was only until I was over 30 years old before someone gave the proper diagnosis. Prior to that, I just knew to fix my face when in meetings or among strangers who wouldn't know how to read me correctly. Often, over the years, people thought I was mean. Later, that'd be like, "You ARE cool."

I made it to my car and let out a deep breath, still in shock as I recalled why I was leaving the parking lot at this time of the day. It felt weird, different, as if

I was in an unknown environment. It was an amazingly sunny day. I looked up and around me and took in the scenery, but instantly the beauty faded as my mind went back to what I'd recently discovered. I cranked up the car and thought, *My life is over.* I'd lost my husband. Just like that. It hadn't even been two years. We didn't make it. How fucking sad was this? My eyes began to leak all over again.

Before I made if two blocks, my phone rang. It was my mother-in-law (MIL). What could she want? I really don't want to talk right now, but she normally didn't call this early for nothing. After a few rings, I finally picked up. "Hello."

"Hi, babe. How are you?" she asked.

"I'm fine," I said in a monotone voice, which wasn't my usual with her. We usually had upbeat voices with one another. Hers was off slightly as well.

"James called me and told me what happened," she went on to tell me.

What? He told his mom? I deeply frowned with confusion. I couldn't believe he called his mom of all people. I would've thought if he called either of them, it would've been his dad, not his mom.

I remained quiet while she talked. "He was upset when he called. I knew something was wrong because it's not like him to call me at this time, and he sounded strange. He eventually got it out that he messed up. He kept saying he messed up. Over and over again. I was trying to keep calm to get him to tell me exactly what had happened."

I jumped in, "Because he did mess up!"

"Yeah, babe, I agree. He did mess up." There was a short paused, and then she asked, "You haven't told anyone have you?"

My whole attitude changed. Is that what the hell she was worried about? Really! Really! She called me because she was so concerned about me making her damn son look bad! Is this what this was about? How dare she! But I should've known. He was her son. He came first. I was not even about to argue with her.

"No, I haven't!" I spat out and left it at that.

"No, I hope I didn't upset you," she explained. "I'm just thinking how when upset sometimes we can say things and sometimes say too much and regret it later. That's all I'm saying."

"No, you are good," I lied.

"Well ok."

I just wanted to get off the phone with her before I ruined our relationship by disrespecting her because she was asking for it, and the way I felt at the moment, I could have given it to her and that was not what I desired to do.

Realizing she had sort of overstepped her boundaries with me, she tried to end the conversation on a good note. "Ok, I'll let you go. I know this hurts, but you know you can call me anytime and I'm there. If you want to talk, call me or let me know, and I can come over. I have no problem with that at all. Ok. I love you like you are my own daughter, don't forget that. Ok."

"Ok," I said. "Love you, too."

I was fuming when I hung up. How dare she call to determine if I'd put MY business out in the streets. None of her business. I could tell whomever I pleased, whenever, and however often I wanted to. Nooo, she was worried I'd tarnish the perfect reputation of that family by letting this one out. No worries, Mother Dearest, I'm not THAT petty. I won't spill all the beans. Sigh.

Home, the house seemed dark even though it was sunny outside and still early in the morning. Not even close to lunch hours. I didn't even bother to open a window for natural lighting, nor did I turn on any switches. I went immediately to get the laptop. I was itching to see if that chick wrote me back. The computer took its precious time booting up. "Hurrrrryyyyy, stupid computer," I said to it.

Once booted, it was still moving a little slow, but I was in. This particular email account was soon to be phased out so not much traffic was on here as it once was. But I could tell I had a message, and I knew it had to be from her. To my surprise, she had the nerve to get smart with me. Wait, wait, let me read this again.

Heart thumping! This trick had gotten smart with me. She basically claimed she didn't know what I was talking about and asked me to leave her out of our business. Oh no, honey, yes you did know what I was talking about, and I dared her to sit here and act all innocent as if I was the crazy one.

So what did I do? Well the obvious. I sent her each of the messages I had that were between him and her. When I sent the first one, I wrote, "See below." On the next one, I wrote, "Here is another one." By time I got a couple more out, my final message to her was, "And what was that you were saying again? You don't know what I'm talking about and to keep you out of our business. Well from these messages, you put yourself into MY business when you started messaging my husband. I wonder if YOUR husband would want to get these, too. I see he is in the global as well. Say another smart ass comment and see what happens!"

I hit SEND and that was that. I dared her to come back with something. I bet I'd send ALL of these to her husband. Bitch, don't play with me!

I know you are wondering how I can remember all of this. Eventually when I returned to work, I couldn't bring myself to delete those emails. Just couldn't do it. You wouldn't have either. Even now, years later and another child later, I still have a folder under another folder (so it's not easily visible) labeled BS (bullshit). No, I don't ever open it. I don't want the reminder, but for some reason, back then, I vowed to keep the evidence so if something ever came out of it, I would have the messages for the lawyers, husbands, mistresses, nosey doubtful mothers-in-law, kids blaming me later on in life, or whatever. I'm sure now I can delete this folder, I just haven't. Not sure why I continue to hold on to such information that could take me down a path of negativity. Well it could've done that back then. I'm so over it now. But still have that folder. I'll delete it. One day.

After I sent that message, I started doing the only thing I knew to do. I went into the garage and got the big black garbage bags we used for yard work to pack up leaves or big items for trash day. I grabbed about four of them and headed to the guest bedroom where James kept his clothes and things. I started with the drawers. Emptying them would be the easiest. After emptying one side of drawers, I went back into the room where I left the laptop and refreshed my browser. I was anxiously waiting on my message back from HER. But nothing was there.

He called. What did he want?

I answered, "What!" Not the normal pleasantries by far. Usually it was "Hey babe." But not now. Not for him.

He started borderline screaming into the phone. "Please stop it!"

"STOP WHAT?"

"Stop writing her. Please stop writing her. Don't do this. Leave it alone. Please."

I couldn't believe that was why he called me. This motherfucker was crazy. "NO, you tell that bitch to stop it! Don't be calling me asking me to stop nothing. I wouldn't be messaging her if it wasn't for your ass in the first place. YOU caused this, so you can get off my motherfucking phone with that!"

He started back up again, but this time with an exaggerated voice, "Nakia, I'm the one you should be upset with. Not her. Please just leave it alone. Please."

"Let me tell you something. I went to her with respect. She is the one who lied to me and told me to keep her out of our business. I don't appreciate her lying. Just like I told her ass, if she says one mo' smart thing to me, her husband will be getting those messages, too. Y'all should've thought about that when you were talking about us behind our backs. So don't call me with this mess. Call her and tell her ass she better watch her mouth because I'm the wrong one to be playing with!" And I hung up the phone.

I was packing his clothes and walking through the house cursing out loud now. I couldn't believe he had the audacity to call me and ask me to stop messaging that bitch. "You tell that bitch she better come at me correct!" I said out loud. I continued talking to him even though he wasn't on the phone. "I don't know who you think I am. I don't play that, but you better be glad I'm not a messy hoe. That is what you better be thankful for. I could fuck up your whole life, mister!"

I stopped and talked to so theatrically you would've thought someone was there in the house with me. My arms were everywhere, facial expressions on point. I mean I was getting all the frustrations out to the darn couches and chairs I guess. All they needed was popcorn. I continued to serve out loud, "I am not the one, dude! I am not the one you want to be fucking with." I clapped my hands together as I talked. "I am not the one. Don't mess up your life fooling with me! You better check that bitch, not me." I paced and exclaimed, "Let her say something else. I dare her behind. Say something else, bitch, and see what happens." I burst into laughter. "Y'all done messed with the right one. That's for sure! Try me. That's all I want. And Imma show both of y'all just who you are messing with."

I had resulted to mumbling: "Motherfuckers got me fucked up. Say something else. I dare you." Sigh. "Motherfuckers."

As I returned to packing up his things, I remembered that I had his keys to the house. Time to change the locks. I paused for a moment to realize the realness of this situation. I shook my head at the disbelief in it all. I called the locksmith I used on my rental property. They'd be out in about an hour and half. Back to the packing I went.

I continued to empty the contents of the drawers into the bags. As I filled one up, I transferred it to the living room to give me space. Goodness, he had more things than I expected. Before long, I had to make another trip out to the garage for more bags. There was still so much more to pack in his closet. And all these shoes. Geez, Louise.

To my surprise, the doorbell rang. It hadn't even been 45 minutes. The locksmith must be early.

I checked the peephole. It was not the locksmith at all but one of my co-worker/friends. Well, she actually worked for me, but I still referred to all of my employees as co-workers because I just didn't have it in me to label them as my employees or to label me as their supervisor. Still to this day, this was hard for me. I really need to work on this. Sorry for the commercial break, but this is something I need to work on even today. There is not a man I know with this issue. But anyhoo.

She was there to check on me. My boss, her second line supervisor, knew of our working friendship and asked her to check on me. He didn't tell her what was wrong but asked her to check on me. This was evident as she walked in and noticed all the filled garbage bags. She glanced around and said, "Hey, I was going to call, but the way his voice sounded, I thought it was best that I came by here to check on you. Are you ok? What can I do?"

Yes, she and I were close. We were close as co-workers before I became the supervisor and even with everything going on, I trusted her. She was my girl in Christ. She prayed for me and would give me the shirt off her back. Even though we normally hid such things, I knew I could tell her, and it not become world news. She was surely shocked. But never did she tell me what to do. She made sure to confirm her ability to do anything I needed her to do. Kept reminding me that she was here for me and asked if I wanted to go seek help, not by myself, but with James. Infidelity is very hurtful, but she said we might need help to assist with how we move forward with the baby. Trey was barely 6 months. The thought of that made my eyes tear up.

To keep her from seeing this and the situation becoming an emotional mess, I turned quickly and started reaching for the bags, not sure what I was going to do with them. "All I know is that he just has to go right now," I started to explain. "I don't know what to do. I just don't know. He just has to get out of here for now while I figure this all out." I moved the bags from one side of the room to other. There was no purpose in what I was doing. I was just trying to move about to help keep my composure in front of her. Yes, we were cool like that, but I was not one to let others see me vulnerable. It was hard to express my feelings to her because I knew if I did, my faucet would turn on and might not turn off. So, I gave her enough to know that I was good for now. Well as good as I could be.

She was preparing to leave, and I reassured her that I would scream if I needed assistance with anything. After she left, I really started to move the bags. This time to the garage until James came by to get them. As I dropped them off into their new closet as they waited for their owner to transport them to another new closet in their new home, I began to cry again. I wished I could just sleep this off and wake up to someone else's life. But I couldn't. This was my life. This was the one I signed up for without even realizing what I was signing up for. I didn't deserve this. At least I didn't think I did. I was good to that man. I was damn good to him, and this was how he repaid me. With cheating on me and destroying our family with our second anniversary coming and a baby.

Congratu-fucking-lations!

7
It's Over Just Like That

Sometime after dark, he sent me a text about coming to get his things.

My reply was simple, "It's all in the garage. Let me know before you come."

Riddle me this. Why was I nervous about the thought of him coming over? Maybe because just that morning, he wouldn't be asking if it were all right for him to come home. Sigh. What had I done? Well first stupid, you kicked the cheater out. This was the part that hurt. I knew what he did. But I still loved him. How does one erase those feelings despite of the circumstances? They don't. And I couldn't. I wouldn't even try, but I would try to focus on exactly what he did so I didn't sit around here and confuse myself. But when he got here, I would ask him about this mess, and I would not let him turn this around on me. You know men are good for doing stuff like that. That'll make you feel like you are the one who was cheating when they get done throwing the blame. No sir, not with me. I didn't make you fall into the trick's bed.

Here was the thing that I had to remember. He was also playing up on another one, this cute girl. Let me do the math for you. There were actually three girls involved who might have had or were close to having sexual relations with this man I married. There's the one that sent her cookie to him on that picture right before we were to marry. Remember that? So, I must ask him about her. Then the one I knew he was actually screwing, the ugly chick. And this new one whom he was emailing to plan to meet out of town. This was the same one he met her after work outside her job. When I was on his computer, he swore they just were talking inappropriately. Explained that nothing happened. But he was a liar, so I would double back to make sure of that. The one who sent him that picture wasn't in town, so there was a chance he hadn't gotten with her lately, meaning while we had been married at least.

Just thinking about all of this made me realize just how stupid I'd been. Call me stupid Nakia. All these degrees and don't have common sense. You see, way back then when he claimed to be venting to this "lady" at work, I didn't approve of it, but that was about it. I thought nothing else of it, and you know why? Because she was ugly. I'd looked her up and noticed that she wasn't all that. James used to have a huge crush on me, and I knew I looked better than this chick. Surely, he wouldn't have touched her. But sad stupid me, I had no clue that she was exactly what turned him on. Silly of me to think looks had something to do with a man's cheating spirit. I'd heard plenty of times how the other woman wasn't attractive, and here I fell for the same thing. Oh well, no sense in beating myself up over being stupid. He would be here soon, and that would be my chance to ask about it all.

I went to check in on Trey as he slept, and after looking into my son's precious face, I whispered a prayer for him and for me. "Lord, I. Need. Help." The tears surfaced again. "I don't know what to do, Lord. Please help me. I have this baby to care for. I know I can do it, but I never imagined I'd have to do it by myself. Help me to understand this. Help me to move on. I know it's early, but I need to heal fast because this hurts sooo bad!" I bellowed as the tears flowed uncontrollably. I went into my bedroomed and sobbed into my pillow. There was nowhere else to store all of these tears. I was already sick of crying, but I couldn't stop. This. Hurt. So. Bad!

I lay there until I was reduced to sniffles and just let my body relax and my mind go off into space. I wasn't not sure how long I was there, but eventually, I was stirred back into conscious when my phone rang, announcing that James had arrived. I shut Trey's door to his bedroom so we didn't disturb him as I walked to open the front door. I barely glanced up, but I noticed that James looked like he just took a beating. I turned away and allowed him to come in as any other stranger through the front door of this house. His house just that morning. Guess we would have to get used to this entry for him since Trey was too small to walk out to his truck for weekend pickups. My stomach churned at the thought of that.

I headed over to the far chair in the room and took a seat while he remained near the side he came in on and took a seat over there. His eyes were fixed on the floor. There was a brief pause. I guess it was on me to start this hard discussion. To my surprise, he began it by saying, "You said you wanted to talk."

Wait. What. How dare he start as if he had nothing to say and that I should get whatever it was off my chest so he could leave.

Agitated, with eyebrows folded into one another, I said, "What?"

He glanced over and spoke with hands gesturing that he came in peace. "No, I'm just saying that you mentioned you had something to tell me. I'm here and wanted to give you the opportunity to get it off your chest. I get it, Nakia. I cheated. At this point, I deserve to hear whatever it is that you have to say. That is all I'm saying. I'm not getting smart or nothing. Just want to give you the chance to say to me whatever you have to say."

I looked off as if to say, "Oh, oh, I thought so." After he explained himself, I let out a deep breath and began to talk. I was so nervous, but I asked him the hard questions. "How many girls have you had sex with?

"Just that one girl."

"Is that the truth? There is the girl that sent that picture to you that I found, this ugly chick that asked you for money that one time, and this new one you trying to meet out of town. Which ones were you fucking? Are there any more?" My courage had returned. Oddly, this reminded me of when I conducted public speaking engagements. Right before I was about to stand in front of a crowd, I got extremely nervous. I would take a deep breath, and once I started talking, the butterflies flew away.

"It was just that one lady you already knew about,"

he said, arm flapping again. "That is the truth. Just her and no one else. The other one I told you the truth, we were just talking. The one who sent that picture was a long time ago before we started talking. We were just flirting when she sent that picture. I'm not saying it was right, but that is what happened. That's it. Just that one girl I cheated with."

It seemed like it took a lot for him to get that out, and as I listened, I believed what he was telling me. I thought I would keep asking questions so I could get all information out of him, and then we could just both move on I guess.

"So, I was right," I said. "She wasn't a lady after all. You made it sound like when you were venting to some lady at work about me that it was an older lady, but actually, she is around your age, and she wasn't no lady. She was your girlfriend."

"No, she wasn't that at all," he interrupted.

Firmly, I stated, "Yes, she was. She was your girlfriend. She has been around for a minute, too. Y'all met before we got engaged. She was even commenting on our photos while we were on our honeymoon. She has been around for a long time. You went to vent to her about me. She had your back." I went in on him hard. Hard to believe I was nervous just minutes ago. "Like I said, she was your girlfriend!"

He didn't respond, so I paused briefly and continued with my questions. "How many times have you all had sex? You said one time, but I know that is a lie. No one gets caught the first time. So how many times?"

"Not like every day or anything like that."

"How many times?" I repeated.

"Maybe once every couple of weeks or so. It wasn't like every week. Just…" he veered off.

"Once every two weeks, like twice a month!? That's a lot!" I stated angrily.

He got defensive. "No, it wasn't like that. You make it sound like all the time."

"Hell, once a month or twice a month is a lot of times! For a man with a wife, that is a lot of times. If it were me, what the hell would you think?"

"No, Nakia. It wasn't a lot of times, just every now and then. I told you the truth. Am telling you the truth. What else do you want me to say?" He had reverted back to his selfish self. The one who thought he had the right to be upset. He had me messed up.

I stood up and let him have it. "First of all, don't get no motherfucking attitude with me! YOU are the one that cheated, not me. Don't get it twisted. YOU owe me the explanations and answers. I can ask all the questions I want, and YOU owe me the answers. If you don't think you do, get the fuck out now because I'm not playing this game of turning the table around on me."

He jumped in. How dare he interrupt me. "Nakia, no one is trying to turn this around. I'm trying to answer your questions. That is why I'm here. That's it. It wasn't a whole lot of times is all I said. I don't want you to think it was like that. I messed up ok! I messed up! I fucked up my family. Ok. I'm not happy about it. But what is done is done, and I'm trying to come clean. That's all I'm trying to do. If it sounds like an attitude, I'm sorry, but I don't know what to do besides just answer your questions. That's it. I messed up. And I'll take full responsibility for what I've done."

He continued, and my eyes started to water again. He was trying to get everything out before he left what had become my house now. So, I let him continue to get it out.

"I know I messed up, and I have to live with that. And I'm willing to do that. I'll stay with my folks for a little while until I figure this out. I'll take care of my son. You don't have to worry about that at all." I could barely see with my tears getting so thick. "I'll keep paying bills around here, so you don't have to worry about that either," he added.

But it was my turn to interrupt because I knew how that mess went. If he paid bills around here, he would think he had control around here and that was not going to happen. No, sir. I wouldn't stand for anything like that.

"No," I replied, "you won't be paying bills around here. I can pay my own bills. You just worry about taking care of your son."

Silence.

I continued the interrogation. "Did you wear a condom each time?"

"YES, Nakia, I'm not stupid!"

"Well, it is obvious you are stupid, so don't say that like I'm crazy. That was a fair question. Now, did you ever bring her here, to this house for sex?"

"No, I would never do that."

"Where?"

"We'd get a hotel," he said.

"So, you were even spending our money on a hotel for the hoe. Unbelievable." Behind me was our, I mean my kitchen. I took refuge there. I wanted my questions answered, but hell, they hurt. In the middle of the kitchen, I stood with my face in my hands. Keeping my sobs quiet proved very difficult, and I had to breathe, so that loud gulp of air let out without my permission, and I carried on crying into my hands until it seemed like I'd gotten it all out. Shaking my head, I thought, I can't believe this. I can't believe this. Whhhhhyyyyy! After I got a little more out, I reached for a paper towel to assault, and then I squared my shoulders back and slowly but confidently went back to the living room where he awaited his verdict.

With a deep, somewhat silent breath, I said, "Your things are in the garage" as I walked past him. "Close up after you've finished, and I'll come lock the door." I retreated to my bedroom.

After he left, I really didn't know what to do with myself. I fidgeted around the house doing a little of nothing. I decided to get my clothes ready for work. The phone rang, and to my surprise it was my father-in-law (FIL). He was a normal man who didn't waste many words. I hesitated to answer because he and I didn't talk about much. We chatted with each other. My MIL and I talked often and shared secrets, and from her call earlier to protect her son, surely that was not what his dad was calling to do.

I answered hesitantly, "Hello."

"Hi, Nakia. This is Dad. Ummm, I'm just calling to check on you. I've talked with James, and I, ummm, I don't know what to say. This is one of those hard situations, and ummm, I just don't know. It's not right, but I know you have the right to do what you want to do, and ummm."

I interrupted him, trying to make this call a little

less stressful for him. "Yes, Dad, it is hard. He cheated! I wasn't enough for him. Period. That's it. He sits around here and doesn't touch me, and now I know why. He wanted someone else. I have to live with the fact that he wanted someone else!" I was speaking loudly and as a matter-of-fact as if my FIL was to blame. After I noticed my tone, I corrected it. "No worries though. Please don't worry. I'm not the kind of person that would keep your grandchild away from you. I won't do that. No matter how I feel, I'll never keep Trey away, so please don't worry about that. I don't know what the future holds, but I'll remain fair and mature about all of this. I promise."

With a softer voice, he said, "I'm sorry for everything that has happened. I truly am. Just know that we are here for you. Anything you need, don't hesitate to call. We are family, and we love you."

Through silent tears, I replied, "Love you all, too."

And we hung up. In my closet, I sobbed yet again. This was what my life had become. Tears and more tears. When would they stop!? I was tired of crying all the time. Lord! When would they stop?

Sleep didn't come easy, but it was necessary to function at work the next day. With the TV on in the background, it was hard to focus on any show for more than 10 minutes. It was like I was literally telling my eyes and brain to focus. It worked for a little while. As soon as the commercial came, it was over. And if I didn't realize that I had reverted back to the inside walls of mental space out there somewhere, even when the show returned, I was still lost in space. By the time I noticed, the show was over and another one was coming on. Ok, time to try this again.

During this time, Trey still needed to be fed during

the night. His first feeding was around 11:30, so I thought to stay up for it and then really try to crash afterwards. Sleep had never been a problem for me. I can sleep anywhere. In cars, planes, in waiting areas (don't matter whose), meetings, etc. Most people say they can't sleep on planes. Shoot, I start dozing off when the plane is taxiing down the runway. I miss all lift-offs, that's how great a sleeper I am. So of course, I might have some No-Doz in the house, but definitely not anything that would help me to sleep. I wondered if I had any Benadryl.

Mama bear heard the stirring going on in the next room. It's amazing how your ears become super sensitive after you have a baby. I can hear him whimper in my deepest of slumber. This was a fear of mine during pregnancy. I knew how easily sleep came and how deeply I'd get, so I feared not hearing him. No sir, no, ma'am; the gift of hearing him no matter what did bless me. So before he can even get the real cry out, I'm already at his crib with bottle in hand. Trey is a good sleeper like Mommy, too. We literally just lay him down, eyes still opened, and shortly thereafter, he is knocked out.

I picked him up and kissed his cheeks. Baby cheeks have a magnet within them, I'm convinced of it. I sat in the rocking chair next to his crib. Positioned him just right in the crook of my arm and began to feed him. Lord, he was so precious. I could stare at this face forever. I began to thank God for blessing me with this child. Then in the middle of the prayer, I was reminded that I had sent his daddy away. I prayed some more. "Lord, please help us." I didn't want to start all that crying in front of him, so I kept the prayer super short and tried to enjoy this precious moment with him. He was such a sweet baby. Yes, he was.

Ironically, the morning came before I knew it, and I was refreshed. I know, right? Look at me, getting some sleep. Go, Kia. Thankful for the little things. And like normal, I was not super ahead of time, so I really didn't have time to think about my situation. I had to focus on getting to work on time, which included getting Trey and myself ready. Getting him ready for Gran-Gran's house was by far the easiest compared to getting myself ready. Since he was just going over to James' mom house, I usually just fed him and put him in his car seat and out we go. She kept clothes over her house to dress him later.

Having my in-laws here in Huntsville had been a blessing to us. My MIL was retired, so we had an agreement that Trey would stay home with her the first year and then we'd enter him into daycare, mainly for socialization. Best decision of my life. It made going back to work and leaving him bearable. I mean I cried like a baby for two of my eight weeks of return to work at the thought of going back to work. Such a shame. I mean cried like a baby at the thought.

Before now, James would drop Trey off because I usually struggled in the mornings getting myself together and I'd pick him up from over my in-laws. It worked because my MIL was a talker. Being the drop-off parent wouldn't help my timing situation because she was hard to ignore. Not that I wanted to ignore her, but I had to get to work and she just wanted to chat about any and everything. I'm sure someone reading this understands. LOL. Love her dearly but the sistah can talk. It worked really well that I picked him up because I didn't mind going in and sitting down and talking for as long as she wanted to. She was really cool though, so I didn't mind talking with her. Heck, she was actually my road dog. With friends with small children, too, it was hard to just say, "Hey, let's go shopping or to lunch" at the drop of the hat. My MIL stayed on ready. We'd spend whole Saturdays together: me, her, and Trey.

But now, I was the drop-off and pick-up parent. Sigh.

We were off. This day would be amazing. I whispered a prayer in the car, "Lord, you know what I need right now. Please guide me. My husband is out of the home, and I don't know what to do. I put him out, but should I have done that? I know we said, "For better or worse," and this is definitely worse. Women forgive cheating men all the time. Am I copping out and allowing him to cheat on me again if I take him back? And why am I even considering this so early? He hurt me, God! And I need Your help. Not man's help. I need to hear from you, Lord. I remember asking You if I should've married him in the first place."

I was getting upset. Less tears, but my tone was harsh. "YOU said it was ok to marry him. YOU gave me the go ahead." As I looked up at the sky, here came the tears. I couldn't do that right now. I'd mess up my makeup.

I let the tears flow for a couple more blocks. A couple minutes later, I remembered to close out the prayer. "I need Your help. Please. Amen."

I tried my best to fix my face before I got to my in-law's apartment. They'd been displaced to this apartment while their house was being put back together from the April 27 tornadoes that destroyed so much in their neighborhood, the infamous Anderson Hills. As the story went, this was the second time Anderson Hills had been hit hard by tornadoes. The first time was in 1996, and James was home when it struck. Luckily, he was in the hallway and in a kneeling position when it came through. From his mom's version, she had just told him to take cover, as he was home alone. He listened and after he did, a boulder shifted in the walls and passed right over the top of him. Had he been standing in that very spot, it would've been over.

When those same thunderous winds visited on April 27, 2011, we were at their home to take cover in their underground storm shelter. We all left work to retreat there. Underground was the safest place after all. His dad hadn't made it by the time the sirens started going off. We just sat on the couch and acted as if nothing was going on outside. It was just so still. What could be going on? A light drizzle, but then the sirens returned. It was then that James told us to go downstairs. We hesitated, but then he repeated it with force behind his voice as if to say, "I don't plan to repeat myself again." And that was toward me and his mom. We sort of looked at each other and just did what the man said. Put Trey in his car seat, scooped him up with a bucket of formula, several bottles of water, his diaper bag, and a framed picture of him. LOL. No lie. I had on flip-flops, but I bet Trey had all he needed, and my MIL had her favorite picture.

We headed downstairs. There was a twin-sized bed down there along with a few chairs, blanket, and radio. About two minutes later, we heard his dad walking upstairs. Relief fell over all of us because we didn't know where he was. Whether he was at work or still driving toward home.

He joined us, and all was well. Until…

Less than five minutes after his arrival, this whistling started above us. Was that the wind? The door of the storm shelter slammed shut. Holy cow! "It's in the house" is what I thought immediately. It was here. The lights flickered off, and the whistling got louder. Everything was quiet except for my MIL repeating over and over again, "The blood of Jesus, the blood of Jesus, the blood of Jesus…" Then all fell silent. Lights came back on. We just sat there not knowing what to say or to think. No one moved. Not even baby Trey. He was only four months at the time, and even he knew to remain quiet. It's like he knew something wasn't right and he dared not to say a word, matching our behavior. My FIL turned away from us and headed up the stairs. All you heard from him was, "Oh gosh!"

My in-laws had been in this apartment since the storms, and this was great for me because it was on the way to work instead of me having to drive further away from the city to get to their house, which took me out the way to drop him off. This was going in the right direction. Oh trust, I never complained about going out of the way. I'd drive to Tennessee and back for this same kind of comfort they provided for my baby. The storms were terrible, but this side effect turned into a blessing. The apartment was no comparison to their big house on the hill, but it put them in a more convenient location in the middle of a new area of the city on the border of Huntsville and Madison. Anything they could ever want was within a few minutes' drive. It broke up their normalcy for just a short period of time and gave them new light. They were there over a year, but I think it was a great place, especially when you've been one place for so many years. Yes, I'm that person. I can find the silver lining in a dark cave. Smile.

Even now, dropping him off wouldn't make me super late as long as my MIL didn't spark up a conversation. But under the current situation, amazingly, she had nothing to say. When I went to the door and knocked, she simple grabbed him up and didn't say much outside of "Good morning," "How are you?" and "Ok." She didn't appear as if she was acting funny with me. I truly believed she was hurting, too. From the call last night from my FIL to the look on her face, even my constant tears...we all were hurting. I was sad at the thought of this. Even though it was not my fault, I still hated what had become of us in such a short period of time. Lord, help us!

As a supervisor, my days are normally busy at work, and this day was no different. I was glad about that as it didn't give me time to reflect on my situation nor time to get sad about it. At work, I was my old self. Happy even. I knew this feeling would be short lived. I had to go home and face my real life after work. I was not looking forward to that, but for now, I'd enjoy being in the right now. For now.

The day flew by, of course. I picked up my son like always, but this time, I couldn't go in and chat with my girl (my MIL). It was not that type of party anymore. I put in the code to get in the gate. Everything looked familiar and normal, but it was not our norm. I parked in front of their building, pulled out my phone, and texted James to let him know that I was outside. A couple minutes later, he emerged from the apartment with our son in tow. His head was down, and I tried to look away. This wasn't what I signed up for, but let the co-parenting begin. He opened the door behind me, snapped Trey into the base of his car seat, and it was over just like that. He walked back toward the apartment. We didn't say anything. I backed out of the parking space, and here came those damn tears again. Along with this godforsaken empty feeling of despair.

My heart was aching. This was my new life, and I didn't like it at all. Picking up my son and leaving without words. I hadn't spoken to James all day. How was this supposed to work? Suddenly, I was supposed to forget all about him. Forget the love we shared. Just forget it all just like that with a snap of my fingers. Who was I going to text throughout the day or send an email to? I now had no one to chat to. Cook for. Lay up against. My bed was now empty, and it would remain empty. No warm body there. It was like someone you love going to prison. They were out there in the universe, but you couldn't get to them. They were off limits. That was what this was, and I didn't like it. You hear. I didn't like this at all. Now the choking sobs had entered the car. Lucky for me, Trey was too young to know what was going on. He wasn't alarmed by my wailing. It meant nothing to him. Little did he know just how much this affected him and the rest of his life. It was not fair!

8
Breaking the Code

Trey was an infant; therefore, I could get away with disconnecting with him for a little while. I was not myself, and I had no reason to fake it. I took care of his basic needs, but I was able to mentally check out and have my mental attention elsewhere. Trey was enjoying his Nick Jr. evening shows after his dinner. I was not very hungry, so after I fed him, I Googled things about what I was going through. Keywords like cheating husbands, how to survive infidelity, moving on from cheating husbands, and should you forgive your cheating husband.

One article caught my attention. The author stated that the first thing most women who are cheated on do is put the man out. She explained that was the biggest mistake we could make. Wait. Really. Now how was I wrong for putting his behind out? I continued to read. She added that cheating was normal and just because a man cheated didn't necessarily mean the relationship had to end. Many people make mistakes, both men and women, she continued. Finding out what drove them to that behavior was key. If the person was a good person, she stated, you could get past this situation and continue on with a successful marriage. But it couldn't be done when the cheater was away. She explained that being away only complicated the issue because no one was truly working it out as they could be if they were in each other's presence.

I took all of that in and read some more articles. Spent the entire evening contemplating what she said along with other authors, but that particular article stood out the most. Did I want to forgive him? Did I play a role in this? Did I still love him? Did I want my husband back? Did I want to work on this with him? Most importantly, did he want to be back? How remorseful was he? Would he continue with these relationships?

The answers to these questions could be hard to hear, but they must be answered. Starting with the ones directed to me. I wanted to forgive him and move on, but only if this would stop. There was no way in hell I was going to settle for a cheating husband. If I took him back, was I settling? Was I giving in too easily? Well, I had better figure this out soon because apparently I was wrong for putting him out. I could very well push him further into the arms of that other woman. But I didn't want to move too prematurely and this turn into something else. I didn't know what to do.

My eyes began to squint. Thoughts had surfaced. I recalled that Sunday service at church where God promised me that James and I would eventually be in church together. He said that we'd worship together as a family and to not worry. Wait. Now I was upset. I began to fuss at the ceiling, "YOU said to not worry because we would worship together. Well, how can we if we aren't together? Why would you tell me to marry this fool? Huh? Why would you then later tell me we will be under one church roof as a family? Why would you allow us to go through this? How can those things happen now? Huh, God!?"

Those blasted tears. ARGH! I was sick and tired of all of this. He promised me. He promised me that we would be all right. Then why was I sitting here crying my eyes out, and my husband was away from me? He cheated on me. He didn't want me. He couldn't want me. How was this being ok? I was not ok. God, you promised me! You promised me!

I was not about to keep doing this. I decided to go to sleep. I must sleep this night away. I couldn't cry all tonight. I just wouldn't do it. I was going to give Trey his bath and prepare him for bed. Afterwards have a glass of wine. That's better than Benadryl. Then I was going to bed. I refused to spend another night in agony.

In bed, I had stopped crying and was very relaxed. I should've thought to have this wine the night before and put an end to all of this. I had the solution for the next time. Just a regular glass. Nothing heavy. I wasn't trying to form any bad habits behind this mess. I just wanted to sleep it away. I was the queen of moving on, right? I'd succumb to this bad behavior for the time being. Give myself a couple weeks and the hard part should be over unless I decided to forgive him. That last part made my heart jump. I could end all of this grief. I could. I could change my narrative and forgive him, right? I could call all this agony quits and call my man back. But...but wasn't that giving in? What lesson would he learn if I decided to do that? I'd just find myself being cheated on all the time for the rest of my life. I couldn't do that. I know many women do it, but I was not them. I was me, and I couldn't do that. I had to stand strong. He couldn't think he could get away with this. I was not to be played with. I could end this pain, but if I did, it could cause more pain for me in the future. Fuck that.

The morning had come. Yay, thank you. The morning was here, and I could return to work and again back to my peace zone of no pain. I'd never been so excited about going to work. I dropped Trey off and off to work I went. I was actually in a good mood. For the rest of the drive, the radio was on low, and the atmosphere felt so serene. I thought about my situation but instead of being sad, I was comforted. My mind wandered back to my thoughts of the night before, but instead of fussing out loud, I just took it all in. God did promise me that what I had been praying for would come true. I know He did. I had been praying about my family worshiping together. So what did that tell me? God was not a man that He should lie. I believed His promise back then and told myself that I would stand on it and be quiet about that subject of attending church together. And I did that. Now, we were at a different fork in the road, but He promised me.

God and I had been cool for some time now. I didn't discover Him in my adulthood as many people have. For instance, most parents drug their kids to church and in return, many of those kids, when they were halfway grown, they veered away from the church as an act of rebellion. They could do what they wanted to do so the first thing off of the list was attending church.

That wasn't my story. I didn't grow up in the church from being dragged there. I grew up in the church on my own. My parents didn't attend church back then, so my introduction to Him to didn't start in my home. I was actually introduced to Him by my aunt. As kids, most were blessed to have family or close family friends with kids that afforded many weekends away at their homes. This was my weekend stay away. When I spent the night over my aunt's house, I was expected to go to church with them on Sunday. Even though I was young when I realized the magnitude of who He was (maybe age 9 or 10), I enjoyed going to church with them. They even invited me to Vacation Bible School weeks.

God often talked to me. As a child, if I ever felt alone or mistreated or down, He talked to me. His spirit was always there comforting me. I can't explain it. He was there keeping me. He encouraged me so much that I promised when I got older, I'd take myself to church. Yes, as soon as I got a car, I'd take myself every week. And I did just that. But before that, as I became a teenager, I used to ask my dad to drop me off at church. He was a great stepdad. He took me to church each Sunday without any issue. My grandmother didn't stay far, and he was a true family man that enjoyed spending time with them. He'd visit them while I was at church, and promptly at 1p.m., he was outside waiting for me. I appreciated him for that. We held that routine for a couple years until I was blessed with my very own new car. I kept my promise and still keep it today.

How do I know it was Him promising me that and

not myself telling me what I wanted to hear? It just was. I didn't make it up, nor can I explain it, nor will I try to justify what I know I heard. He promised me, and I had to have faith and rely on it, just like that other time I trusted Him and moved to Atlanta. After I graduated from Jackson State University, I didn't have a job waiting on me to start. Didn't know I was even supposed to be applying for jobs ahead of graduation. I'm just being honest. No one told me to do that, so I hadn't done it. So, I continued to work at the bingo hall that summer after graduation while looking for a job. I wanted to live in either Atlanta or Dallas. Seemed like everyone wanted to same thing.

I'd apply for different jobs and made turnaround trips back and forth to Atlanta for interviews. I wasn't getting many calls from Dallas. Eventually, one week, it came across my spirit to just move. Instead of driving back and forth, go there and stay and look for a job. But where would I stay? I had a best friend from high school there, but she was married with kids, and even I knew to have sense enough to not barge in on them. Then it struck me. She also had a sister there, and we were somewhat cool. For a person who rarely asks for help, it amazes me just how comfortable I was with approaching this subject of moving in. She said yes. I promised to pay her $100 a week, go half on groceries, and of course to keep her house clean.

In hindsight, it was His voice leading me and testing me to see just how cool we actually were. I know that now as it was less than two weeks that I left for Atlanta. Gave my job a week's notice that I was leaving. No money for real. No plan. All I knew was that I was going to Atlanta for a job. The Sunday before I left (was leaving the following Monday), I stopped by my aunt's house to let her know that I was leaving for real. Needed to see her before I'd left. She had company at the house.

It was a lady from 'our' church. Shady Grove was my church now. I'd been baptized and everything over the years. She heard my talk of leaving and told me that she had two brothers, both crazy JSU alums, and both active as either president or vice president of their own local JSU alumni chapters. One brother lived in Atlanta and the other one in Birmingham. So of course, when I got to Atlanta and settled in, by Tuesday I was calling the brother in Atlanta. Time out for being shy. I needed a job and needed one soon. He didn't answer, so I called the one in Birmingham. He picked up. After introducing myself, you'd think we were old pals. He didn't wait. He started calling people on three-way (remember those types of calls?).

One of the people he called was the president of the JSU alumni chapter in Huntsville, and she knew of an internship that was opening up that Friday with the Department of Defense. Smile. I applied and have been working for the government 15 years to the date of writing this book. Look at God.

I concluded that if He could speak to me and tell me to leave my home and everything I know without fear, surely He could speak over my marriage. I know what I heard. He spoke that it was ok to marry this man just as He promised we'd worship together. And I would rely on His promises. If Abraham could raise a knife in the air, surely I could forgive this cheating. My husband must come back home. We had some work to do.

I was in the car line at the gate when I texted

James: "If we are to work on this, you need to be at the house with us working on it. If you don't want to work on it, just say the word, and I'll understand." I showed my government badge to the gate guard and proceeded to my building. My phone beeped, indicating I had a message. It was James. "You sure you want me home?"

I texted back: "I said what I said. If we are to work on this marriage moving forward has to be done at home, not away."

"Ok."

I continued to drive. But now, I felt just a bit more confident. My day was bright. Seemed like the sun just came out. Wow. I immediately began to feel better. It didn't hurt as bad. Yes, he cheated and that wasn't right, but God made me a promise, and I was selfish. I wanted everything He had for me. I wouldn't give up now. I'd come too far. I didn't get this husband to let him go that easily, especially with God's promise lurking in the bushes. I couldn't let Him down. I couldn't let my marriage down. And I wouldn't fail my son. James and I were meant to be. I didn't care what anyone said—even though no one really knew at the time.

I was going to fight through this. God was up to something.

After work, instead of picking up Trey, I texted James to bring him home when he came. I didn't want to face that awful pick up again. I went home and prepared my house for their return, thanking God the whole drive. It was all due Him. Glory and Honor. I knew we would be ok now. I just knew it.

Throughout the day, I searched for things that

would help me start forgiving. Things to help set boundaries. I would not stand for this cheating, so I had to make sure I did this right. Counseling was a must! Period. He had to agree to go to counseling. No more secrets. That extra email account was gone from the last confrontation, but now, we couldn't have passwords. I would insist. No locked phones, and we both had to give up the passwords to these email accounts to include Facebook. Roll your eyes all you want, I said what I said. If I was to move on like nothing happened, it would be on my terms. I didn't screw this up, he did.

I was still not that girl. The one who was insecure about everything. I didn't plan to stalk his accounts. That wasn't my intention. I wanted to be sure we didn't continue such easy access to the outside world without considering the other person. He wouldn't be inboxing anyone on FB if he knew there was a chance I could see it. And yes, I knew I couldn't pop up to his work again like that, checking his emails. Even after finding this out, I didn't want to resort to that kind of behavior. It just wasn't me. I just wanted the luxury of checking his accounts from time to time until I was more confident in our marriage. You don't have to agree. I'm not married to you.

After Trey was put to bed that night, James and I talked so we'd both know what to expect of each other and how we should move forward.

"Are you ready to talk?" I asked.

I was sure he was expecting this, but it still took him off guard. "Sure." He sat, and I took a seat on the other couch. Didn't realize how nervous I'd gotten. Now how do I say this? I was afraid to start.

After a couple of minutes, he looked over and

said, "You wanted to talk. I'm listening."

Wait. Was that, that attitude again? Had he not learned? Come on, Nakia. Don't read into this, tell him what you are after. If he doesn't agree, he knows where the door is.

"I did want to talk," I said as a matter-a-fact. "I'll just get it out since you are rushing me."

"I wasn't trying to rush you."

I proceeded as if he wasn't talking. "You was. But anyway. If we are to move on and work on this marriage, I have a couple demands. Meaning things that must take place." I paused to catch his reaction. He looked over at me like he questioned me. I tilted my head to the side with puffed out lips as if to say, "I didn't stutter." Then I continued. "We must go to counseling and get some help." Pause. He didn't say anything. "OK?" I said as if to say, "You heard me."

"Ok, Nakia."

"Don't ok Nakia me!" I rolled my eyes. "And no more secrets. I want all the passwords to your email accounts, your Facebook, and there should be no passwords on our phones." Pause. "And I'll give you my passwords as well. No secrets. Nothing is to be a secret between us. I don't want to be in your accounts all the time, but I need access to check periodically if I need to. No secrets. If we go to counseling and share this info, we can go forward." Pause. "Ok?"

He sighed. "Yeah, Nakia. Ok. Whatever you say. We can go to counseling, and you can have all of that other stuff if it will make sure I don't have this thrown in my face all the time."

"What!"

He continues, "I know you, Nakia. You ask for all

of this, and if I give it, you will still throw this up in my face, and I don't want to deal with that all the time. I know I fucked up, and I want my family back, but I don't want this to become a constant thing for us."

I jumped in, not having none of this talk. "First of all, remember this, YOU are the one who stepped out, so don't be up in here telling me what I bet not do. If I have to bring it up, I will do just that. Yes, I want to forgive you and move on. I don't care to be talking about this either, but if it comes up, it comes up, and you will just have to deal with it. You can't tell me to shut up about it if it's bothering me. That's not fair. And I'm not agreeing to it. So come again."

He was silent. We both were. I took this as a chance to restate what I wanted. "James, this hurts like you will never know. I want to forgive you and work on my family, but we must have boundaries that neither of us can cross or cross again. I can't deal with this cheating. Is this something you think you will do again?"

"NO, Nakia. I hate I got caught up and did this to you. I really am. I fucked up. Ok. But I love you, and I love my son. I want my family. We can go to counseling. And I'll give you my passwords. I'm sorry. I fucked up. I just want my family back." His voice cracked a little, and my eyes filled up with tears. It was a different kind of cry this time. He was hurting, too. Even though he caused this, he was hurting, and I wanted to go over and comfort him. I couldn't help who I was. I was a woman. We feel pain when others hurt, but I couldn't will myself over there. So, we just

sat there in silence. A couple sniffles came from his

direction. I wiped my nose.
Peace came over the house.

9
Road to Recovery

James handed over his usernames and passwords, and I did the same. I put them away at my desk at work. But not before snapping a picture and emailing to my personal account, but then I remembered he will have access to this account as well. He might get to snooping around and see it and think I don't trust him. It's not about not trusting him. I just need the comfort of knowing he won't be that stupid again. Chances are good that he won't use these accounts for his flirting, that I can almost guarantee. Well sure he can use them and delete the messages, but how long will that last? Not long because the other person could send a message that goes unread that I could very well catch before he did.

I am confident in this new rule. Same with his cell phone. Without it having a password locking it up, I can walk by and open it up and look as I please. I don't plan to do this, but I could. His risk of getting caught is extremely high now, so I didn't think he would engage in such things again. No time soon. On these things. I'm not stupid. Nothing is foolproof, and he still has his work computer even though he now realizes he married a lunatic that will show up. His work computer is still the easiest method for doing his dirt. And who is to say there isn't a work wife lurking around that I don't know about? He could have easily been talking to the two girls via email and still have another woman around the office. I'd never know about her, but I can't worry myself with all the 'what ifs' there could be. Nor will I allow myself to go down that negative path of no return.

That path is so easy to get on, but it's a vicious one that will not do us any good. It would be hard keeping it together, but I must do it or else we wouldn't last. I had already spent a whole night going through his accounts. I mean through them. I opened every folder and checked out the conversations within them. I couldn't continue to do that, but now that I'd swept through them, I promised myself to move on. Such behavior was not healthy at all. I didn't want to be that wife. I wouldn't be that wife. I wouldn't. I couldn't.

It was actually James who located a place we could go get counseling. I'm thankful I'm not on this by myself. He knows we need help. We agreed that we wouldn't take this to the church. For one, he didn't want to automatically go to my church, and I of course would not agree to counseling from his church, so we agreed that our counselor needed to be independent of either church and whomever we choose, we couldn't know them because we didn't want any biases.

Black folks usually consider counseling as being

only for crazy people. Glad that stereotype isn't us; however, it makes it difficult to get a recommendation from our friends or family due to the stigma attached. They will assume we are either about to lose our minds or that something is seriously wrong with the marriage—which it was. We knew it would be difficult to ask for a recommendation and then find out that they didn't have one because then questions would come. They would want to know what was going on with us, and if we didn't tell, they would make something up on their own. Huntsville is small. Our true business or the made up one will get around, and that was not what we wanted, so we didn't ask around.

He set the appointment. His parents agreed to pick up the kids from school on those days. They were our only confidants at this time. They'd do whatever we needed without question that's for sure. Our time was set for the very next week; no time to waste, no time to talk ourselves out of it, and I was glad for the expediency.

Our first appointment was standard. We filled out paperwork for the lady, and she basically reviewed our entries to better understand the purpose of our visit. This was my first time in such a space, and it looked nothing of how it does on TV. No huge couch for us to sit on. This place is basically a home converted into a counseling center. The room was once someone's bedroom, small and quaint, but the waiting room tells me it isn't new or unused; therefore, we won't judge it based off of size and splendor, or lack thereof.

I didn't expect to cover a lot on the first day, and

she didn't disappoint. The first appointment was a meet and greet type of session, but we did get to the big issue, his infidelity, slightly. Through the unfamiliarity of such meetings, I was glad to have it end with my anticipation being for the future appointments when we could arrive and everything being as we last left it the previous time. Our arrival being more welcoming versus awkward with a 'hi Amy,' 'hi James,' and 'hi Nakia.' Yes, please bring on those times.

We departed unchanged, but our next session was in a couple days. Twice-a-week sessions on Mondays and Wednesdays. I was thankful. If this had been once a week, I probably would have twins each week in between those sessions. That would be way too many days in between and we'd forget what we last discussed. So, I guess these people know what they are doing. Outside, James walked me over to my car to discuss who was going to pick up the kids. I agreed to grab them. There was an uncomfortable pause before he asked if I was ok with what we just did, and I confirmed to him that I was fine with it all and was looking forward to more sessions. He agreed. We looked at each other for a moment and then he proceeded to his truck. Just like that. We were on our way to recovery. This road wasn't designed to be easy. It would be scary at times, but I was glad we were on it together, and we both were trying to get better for one another.

For that, I whispered, "Thank You, God."

This was our routine for the next few weeks, but we surprisingly were given a new counselor after two weeks. The one we had was moving out of state. Well, ok, I thought. One would think they would let you know this prior to your arrival, but I guess had they told us we would have to come in and start over with another lady, chances were great that we would consider not returning based off of the change. People don't like change, so I respect their decision to not share that bit of information. And it's a good thing that she wasn't around long enough to upset us with such an abrupt change.

The new lady was very different. To our surprise, she was handicap. She was blind, well sort of blind. She had a help dog and everything. The dog was in the room with us. Talking about uncomfortable, but I tried not to question this. Her handicap didn't have anything to do with her abilities. Keeping our brains in check has got to be the hardest thing ever, especially with so many biases and stereotypes that exist in this world. We have to be honest. We all judge people negatively most of the time without even giving them a chance to open their mouths. Just like the first time we entered this place, just like the first lady we had, we would give this a chance, period.

After getting acquainted with the new lady, I actually liked her spirit. She had a more calming demeanor, and I felt freer to talk with her. She had a more mothering spirit about her, less rushing, and more listening. After the first visit, I felt different, and I like it. I couldn't say the same for him, but I knew this change wasn't initially accepted by him. It is a fact that people don't like change but I'm a little more flexible than my husband, so I prayed this didn't affect our progress.

I can't recall how long we were in counseling or just how we decided to end our sessions, but I can recall this one session that helped us both as we both were in tears at how we had been talking past one another. Things I was doing, he was reading them wrong, and things he was doing, I was misinterpreting. Like who would've thought this was even going on without her bringing it to my attention. I believe that session led to a more in-depth discussion for us.

We were heading to my hometown the weekend following that session. Usually I sleep half the way home and we'd talk a little of the drive. There are even times when we may not talk much at all during the ride. But this time was very different. We discussed that awakening session we'd just had with the counselor that week recalling situations that we apparently screwed up.

One of James' main complaints, that I don't think has ever gone away, is my lack of being aggressive in the bedroom. He has always felt that he was the only one initiating sex, but if you were to ask me, I'd agree that he was the main person but not always. But he is the one that always wanted sex, so wouldn't it make sense that he would be the one starting it? He would never understand my side of this. As a woman, sex is not my top priority in life so why expect me to jump on him on a regular basis is beside me. I do understand his need of feeling wanted, so I do initiate it at times, but he needed to realize that wouldn't match his attempts. Ever.

There is one time I can recall actually trying to be the aggressor. This wasn't easy for me. I mentioned this at the beginning of this book. Remember the time I texted him, 'COME AND GET IT,' and he told me that if I wanted it, I needed to come to him, and I decided it wasn't worth the headache? Well, we discussed that situation and guess what I found out? You will never believe this. He said that he didn't come to me because he felt I was trying to run the situation and that was his way of letting me know I didn't control him. I can't make this up.

Real talk. He explained that he was so used to me trying to control him that he took my advance as yet another way of me trying to have control. In a nutshell, he wasn't for me telling him what to do, so if I wanted sex, I needed to go and get it versus giving him commands. Of course, we had a big laugh about this. With so many miles ahead of us, I was able to explain that I didn't know how to be what we wanted. It wasn't in my DNA, and that each time I tried, it wasn't working. It reminded me of how he turned me down when I literally walked to the bathroom butt ass naked. He admitted through laughs that he was totally wrong for that and didn't know why he'd done that. He couldn't explain it.

I explained how from that I assumed he needed time to get ready for sex. I didn't know why he turned me down. Maybe I caught him way off guard. Heck, I was left to make all the assumptions in the world, including feeling he didn't want me anymore. So that is why I sent that text. I thought maybe he needed notice of booty. Hell, I don't know. It is what I tried and again it didn't work. So what was a girl to do besides give up on it. And that was where we were. I'd given up on it and so did he.

Cheating was inevitable.

I then understood thoroughly how we'd gotten there. I did play a role. Not accepting blame but I'd had a role to play. All the miscommunication. All the failed attempts at initiating sex. Maybe I should've found a friend to talk this over with. A married friend. Or read a marriage book for that matter. But I didn't. Here is the thing. I had all the books in the world (not really but you get what I'm saying) on goal setting, motivation, flipping houses, etc., but hadn't invested in any books on marriage. I even recall reading one book on getting and keeping a man years prior to his arrival called Why Men Love Bitches. That book was so awesome and full of great points that may have actually helped me snatch up James.

So why didn't I think of reading something to help me with my marriage? Well, I think that is the issue with so many of us. We get married and think we have accomplished the goal. That is so far from the truth. Actually, it could be viewed as an abomination to all that we've been taught or learned inadvertently. And I believe this is part of the journey that I'm on. To break down these terrible marriage stereotypes in which we base our marriage on. To teach each of us to learn how to invest in our marriages so we don't continue these vicious failed cycles. To give us tools and methods of investing and ultimately of how to learn to be real and truthful with not only others around us but also ourselves.

To be fake in our homes is a tragedy.

10
Marriage 101

This should've been taught in school, but it wasn't. Just like personal finances was left out. Seems like we forget that basic life skills should be taught right alongside things like Home Economics and Physical Education. Maybe it's because so many of us fail at life that no one dares try to teach it. Maybe it is because we fear failing at it in public with other people standing around judging us. Even with writing this book, I'm setting us up for ridicule. It's far better to be obedient to Him and worry about that than worrying about what the world has to say. The world will always have something to say. I (or we) dare not waste time worrying about the world because as we look around, it doesn't seem to have it together nor are many willing to tell their story. Nor is the world willing to help us with this thing. Forget the world. Put our wages on Him.

One of my fears is of mistakes and failures coming

in my marriage as a result of this book. Me writing this book doesn't vaccinate us from the effects of daily living nor prevents our own personal trials and tribulations. They shall come, that I do know. I hope those reading know we are human and no matter what, we will still face things in our marriage, and it will get hard, and I will fight no matter what. We are still a work in progress. Marriage is not a destination. It's a journey. We are continuing to learn as we go.

We are on this journey of Fighting for Marriages, and so while we help those with our serum, we will allow the Holy Spirit and others around us to assist us as well. We are not immune. The enemy shall come and test us. You'd best believe it will. Just the same, trust that as soon as you decide to follow us and fight for your vows, the enemy will join your journey of fighting as well. That is his (the enemy's) job. I wrote about this very topic before within two blog posts: one called "Free Psychic Helpline" on 11 July 2017 and another one called "FREE Psychic Advice Part II" on 16 July 2017. Here is a blurb from "Free Psychic Helpline":

Everything was going so well until…

Until all hell broke loose around you! Think about it for a second. Think about the last time you confessed to yourself that your blessing was on its way. Think about when you confessed your faith in Jesus Christ as your Lord. He was who you would follow the rest of your days. You were tired of being sick and tired of worldly things. No more fence straddling. You were about to get your mind right!

You see that is exactly when the enemy gets pissed

looking at you. The enemy can't stand to see you walking around smiling for no reason. Can't stand to see you making goals and checking them off. Can't stand to see you with your friends eating out for lunch, laughing, and having a good time. Can't stand your life turning for the better. Like who told you that you had permission to have a life and a life abundantly, he ponders!

Investing into your mind through inspirational messages and surrounding yourself with positive vibes. He growls. He hisses. Eyes become narrow. How dare you tell someone you are blessed and highly favored! Who are you!? His chest goes up and down from heavy breathing. Palms are sweating. Head is pounding. He breaks a broom across a door hinge. His mind is made up. He must destroy you! He must put an end to this new confidence you exude. And so he sets out on his plan to ruin your plans.

Keep that in mind as you fight, but don't fear him and his tactics. I don't know about you, but I serve a God that is bigger and badder. What *could* happen has no place in your heart or in your head. Stay focused on God, and there is very little time to be worried about other trivial things. Don't get me wrong. When things happen to us, it does hurt, and it can be damaging, but it's all temporary. I know you have heard that all ends up turning out for our good. I am a believer and witness that it will turn around and work for us on the other side.

While on this journey, I've become a sermon junkie. Like no lie. Once I realized just what He had in store for me to do and when I began to follow His lead, I knew things would come in my way to prevent His will. Often, the way to fight is not through curse words and swinging of your fist. Sometimes the only way to fight is in the spiritual realm of prayer and fasting. Therefore, before we held our first couples game night, the weeks prior to the event, I went into prayer and fasting. I don't think I would've made it through that period without praying and fasting. This consisted of a couple days of complete fasting (water only) and something referred to as 'dusk to dawn,' where you didn't eat anything until after dark each day.

Once the party idea came to me and my feet got to moving to bring it into fruition, there were about six weeks involved, and I prayed and fasted for half of that time, a 21-day streak of dusk to dawn and am so very proud that I did. To tell the truth, since getting through his infidelity and going to counseling to learn how to operate together, James and I had argued more in that six-week period than we had in the last six years. I kid you not. The fights were coming from everywhere. I can recall watching James pass by me one day in the house, and I glanced up at him and knew then that the enemy had entered the house. And he was. The next day or so, James said something out the way to me, and I said in my head, "Told you so." I just listened, knowing not to feed into whatever it was. Afterwards, in prayer, I asked God how to respond, and all He said was to apologize. Heck, I didn't even know what I was apologizing for, but I did it anyway. Dude texted me, "thanks." I looked up and to the side like "Whatever, whatever it takes, I ain't got no time for this."

I hope not to scare you, but spiritual warfare is REAL. After I got it off of my husband, it didn't leave the house. He was still there. It literally leaped off of James and landed on my daughter. And resided with her, in hindsight, about four or five days. The week of that discovery, she was acting out of character, but I attributed it to the fact that she was just 4 years old. You could get anything out of a dramatic 4-year-old, but this time was different. Very different.

She had just finished getting her braids done. This particular stylist comes to the house to do London's hair. Being in their own environment allows the little girls to be comfortable and less afraid of the process. It had worked before, but this time, she wasn't having any parts of this and cried and screamed just about the entire time. I mean I almost wanted to ask the lady to stop where she was, but I knew that wasn't possible. We got to the last three braids (3 of about 10, like this was a light braid session that took the same amount of time as if she was putting a lot of braids in), and I had to literally hold London down. I wrapped my arms around her as if I was giving her a hug. Her legs, however, appeared as if she was running in place. This turned out to be the worse braiding experience ever, I thought. I felt terrible, but after it was over, she felt beautiful and had forgotten the whole ordeal.

After putting her to bed, I prepared for bed myself. This time I took a break from Bishop Jakes and listened to one of my all-time favorites, the late Dr. Myles Munroe. The YouTube message was titled, "The Truth About You." In it, Dr. Munroe discussed the creation of the earth to include the purpose of Jesus, why God created Him. This led to a discussion of the Holy Spirit as well as the enemy's spirit. It explained how the enemy needs a body to carry its spirit on earth. This is done by getting inside of us and causing us to fulfill his mission. Very eye-opening message. I'd known these things but hadn't heard of it explained in such a manner. Check it out on YouTube when you get time. I actually have that message saved within my YouTube account.

It was almost midnight when I finished that message, took my Bluetooth off, and laid down, realizing just how late it was. I closed my eyes but was awakened within seconds, not minutes, to London's screaming. She was in her brother's bed because she was still too afraid to sleep in her bed. That week we'd started trying to make her sleep in her bed, but since she had such a rough time, I allowed her to sleep with him.

I was almost in a sprint trying to get to his room to see what was wrong. Her eyes were half-opened. To not wake him, I grabbed her to pull her to bed with us. She grabbed his leg, and his head flew up, and when she let go, he went back down to sleep. That was strange. I tried to quiet her down as I carried her to my room. She would definitely be sleeping with us that night, which was fine. I wanted her near me. I was scared because I didn't know what was wrong.

I laid her down between James and I, but she wouldn't be still. She was still tossing and turning. She was a bad sleeper, but she was kicking her legs and everything. She kicked James, and I could tell he was upset, but I tried to let him know that everything was ok and that she was having a bad dream. Maybe night terrors. She'd had those before, but it had been a long time since she had one, and they were never like this. She was kicking and thrusting her body.

With squinted eyes, I stares at her and thought

about the message I just heard. My oil was in my purse just below me on the side of the bed. I didn't even have to get up. I wondered if I should use it. She had been acting strange all week. Monday, she cried like a baby when I dropped her off at school. We'd been over that for months. Wednesday morning, she woke up and told me while I was getting dressed that a monster pushed her while she was in her bed. I told her that she probably saw me come in there and kiss her. She said, "Yes, I know you kissed me, but that wasn't you who pushed me. It was the monster." I'd remembered while in bed with her and knew I must pray over her.

I reached down to the side of the bed and retrieved the oil out of my purse, not taking my eyes off of London. I put some on my index finger and proceeded to mark her head with a cross designed with oil.

But she was kicking and jolting so bad that I had to use my left hand to hold her head still to draw the cross. As I finished drawing the cross, I whispered, "The Father, The Son, and The Holy Ghost," and immediately, her body went limp. Heart pounding. I prayed. I prayed for that enemy to not only to leave my baby alone but also to get the hell out of my house. Through gritted teeth, "GET OUT."

Afterwards, I just sat there staring at her. Sort of expected a sly grin to come upon her face, but it didn't. She just lay there peacefully. Everything about her now had changed. James was softly snoring. I relaxed and joined her. It was time for sleep.

Once I realized the realness of spiritual warfare and the importance or recognizing such warfare, my sermon catalog began to grow. I was addicted to listening to full sermons by Bishop T.D. Jakes. I heard a message that stood out to me about a doctor that was out to cure Eboli. Too cure the disease, the doctor had to inject himself with the virus. So the cure was in the virus itself. This is referred to as serum. Bishop Jakes tagged it as serum solutions. Often in life, bad things happen to us, but that thing ended up saving us.

What James and I went through at the beginning of our marriage hurt like hell, but I know it was our serum solution because after we went through those things, we got so much better. The arguing stopped. At first, we argued almost daily, but then into our third year, it's like all the fighting stopped. I can count on my hands how many fights we had during that time after counseling. I'm not saying counseling was the cure. It did help us tremendously, but we had to take what we learned and learned to apply those things. Through counseling we had to learn how to fight fair. Not the long mean texts or emails. No jumping to conclusions. And we learned how to communicate with one another.

It was in our fourth year that I realized I had a best friend. We could talk about any and everything. We could laugh at it all, including laughing at ourselves. I don't know what we were doing when we first got married. Shoot, besides the marriage license, I can't even confess that we were married. We were just roommates.

From that huge issue, I had a husband I could depend on and trust. I had someone I didn't want to live without. He was my confidant. He was my soulmate. But it took the disease for us to realize what we had with one another. Our very own serum solution. And here we are with the desire to inject every married soul we meet with our serum. Our hope is that no one else has to suffer in silence from this infection that consumes us all from time to time. Nothing wrong with having the flu when you seek help for the proper diagnosis and medicine.

I'm no doctor. Well, sort of. I'm no medical doctor. I don't have to be. What we have doesn't need a prescription. I'm not a marriage counselor. I don't have to be that either. Matter-of-fact, I encourage people to seek their help from time to time. I'm just a witness. I can only help you with what I got. When was the last time someone told the truth about the secrets of their four walls? Not many do or ever will. That is all I have to offer. I heard His voice say, "Tell it." As a result, I will not be afraid. I'll keep telling it and sharing it all while hoping and praying it helps this union called marriage.

Before I lay out strategies I believe are effective, let's discuss some more things like why you don't know these things I'm sharing. Now many of you do. I'm not alluding to us being in the dark or being stupid. What I'm trying to express is how easily it is to forget the things we know to be true because of our emotions, our flesh, our environment (lies all around us), and for the fact that so many of us are so smart that we analyze everything with logic and theory. Bishop T. D. Jakes shared some scientific research in one of his sermons about how basically (I'm paraphrasing) the more intelligent an animal is, the less likely it is to use its instincts. As women and mothers, you know we have good instincts, right? We refer to them as our intuition, and nothing can amount to the level we hold our intuitions on. Well, the smarter we become, chances are great we start to rely more on our intellect to make decisions that deal with matters of the heart. I'm not saying this is wrong, but ummm...yeah. I'll let you determine how successful this has been for you. In the meantime, let's address why this may be new to or forgotten by many of us.

11
The Problem with Being a Selfish Ass

Bet you won't believe me when I say this: some of y'all became the most selfish folks in the world after you married. There, I said it. I dare any of you to challenge me on this. And I was one of you, too. But I'm not now, so I get to point the finger and chastise you. Selfish. Selfish. Selfish. Imagine me wagging my finger at you, too.

No one likes to be told about themselves. And that my friend is issue number one. It goes both ways. I'm not just talking about us women nagging about you guys. Overall, it's a slap in the face when we try to correct each other. Take a look around, particularly on social media sites. Notice when someone tries to share feedback with someone, doesn't matter how constructive it may have been or true, people go on rants to explain how they were wronged?

"How dare my used to be BFF tell me I'm wrong for flirting with her new man. Just because I slept with her last boyfriend doesn't mean I want every man she got. What happened to forgiving a person? Thou shall forgive if we shall be forgiven or something like that. Is that what the Word says? And she call herself a Christian. What a hypocrite!"

Know anybody like that? People who are in the wrong, but as a friend you can't tell them. And what is it that we do? We reply to the post with things like:

Fake friend #1: Hold your head up shawty. This too shall pass.

Fake friend #2: She wasn't never your friend boo. I been told you that years ago. Don't worry. She gone get what she deserve.

Fake friend #3: See that's why I stopped going to the church. They don't practice what they preach and then want all your money.

When we don't get our way, we tend to go around to other friends for support and encouragement of our foolery. With social media having the world's cheapest psychologists on payroll, we automatically go there for the plethora of good, sound advice everyone gives.

Well what does that have to do with what goes on within our homes, within our relationships? It's obvious. The same silly rants we conduct on social media, we showcase in our homes. If someone doesn't know how to conduct themselves on this free application among strangers, family, friends and foe; how do you expect them to act or respond to those in their own homes? No, this isn't an absolute, but it is a good indicator. Whether you are the one posting the message or the one pacifying the messenger, I believe they both are one in the same.

It's a concept referred to as self-awareness. We are often not in tuned with ourselves and the things that we do and portray about ourselves. We don't see any wrong in our actions, yet we are the most 'other-aware' about everyone else. We have no problems pointing fingers at and correcting others' others.

It's human nature. We can't help ourselves. I do it, too, without realizing it at first. But shortly there afterwards, I correct my own behavior. Have you ever done that? Realized you were wrong for your way of thinking and corrected yourself? Never or rarely? I correct myself all the time. Daily corrections. I'm no better than you, but I'm here to say that more times than not, we are the ones who need to point the finger at ourselves.

Let me be sure to add this: it isn't judgment if it's true. Judgment occurs when I determine who you are based off of an action you have done. When I determine your character off of an incident without even knowing you and form an opinion of you prematurely, that's judgment. But if you are a thief, and I say you are wrong for stealing my stuff, hell, you are a wrong thief.

I hate the word judgment because we use it in the wrong manner far too often. We use it to cover up our wrongdoings and as an attempt to justify ourselves. Maybe the real issue is that I said it wrong when I called you to discuss the situation with you. Maybe I should've prepped you first by taking a more softer approach versus being so direct. But my sin from high school still doesn't negate the fact that you are wrong from stealing from me.

No one wants to be accountable anymore for actions. If I tell my husband that he hurt my feelings when he yelled at me, what does that have to do with that one time I raised my voice two months ago? Ever did that before? Instead of owning up to getting out of control, you reach back to expose that person's past wrongdoings. Now the argument has ensued. Both are loud now, and by the end of the fight, the issue is not resolved, and everyone's feelings are hurt.

It's a never-ending cycle. This was the definitely the case for me and James in the beginning. I was always trying to point out his wrongs. I'm not saying I was perfect, but he was the kind of guy who never expressed things to me, so it was always me being the bad guy. I didn't want to get on the other side of this marriage wishing I had told him this or that. I'm sure my approach was all wrong. But when I would attempt to express these things to him, he acted like that was his prime opportunity to put me on blast for things I'd done to him. Next thing you know, we would be fighting and then he'd go into his silent treatment for the next few days.

This wasn't working to say the least. One thing we learned in counseling was the proper way of fighting. Just like competitive boxers, we had to learn the right fighting stance, how our arms and legs needed to be positioned, how to train, and how to shake hands at the end. Real talk. No more fighting over emails or text messages were allowed. No more pointing the fingers but instead we expressed how the action made me feel. More listening and less jumping in. You do realize, most of the time, you check out of listening to form your next defensive counterargument.

I point out these different examples because we all

are different, yet we suffer with the same things. Overall, it boils down to the same thing. When it comes to our most precious commodity, which is self, we miss out on the things self does. We don't hesitate to utter the phrase, "I know I'm not perfect. No one is perfect." But how often do we assess our imperfections? How often do we sit back and think about how these imperfections affect others? Maybe not often. And when people bring these things forth, how do we respond? Do we accept them as our truths with the goal of working on them? Or do we ignore and/or fight with the messenger, denying the truth's existence? How often do we try to change? How does one change something that is so integral to their whole being? How do you change something you had no knowledge of its effects? And when we attempt to change, how do we know that our efforts are working?

One thing I had to do was acknowledge that my husband had his side to this story as well. He didn't express it often, but when he did throw it back in my face at the wrong time, I still had to listen to him instead of denying it. This was difficult at first because it wasn't his turn. It was my turn to vent. But instead of wasting time trying to remind him of this, I just listened and learned to not fall for that trap of going down that rabbit hole with him. Acknowledge his feelings and stir the ship back in the direction I was heading with a softer approach instead of making him get on the defensive.

We both learned too that bringing up old stuff wasn't the proper way to indulge in each other's feelings when approached with concerns or things that bothered the other. We had to learn to be adults and not fight as our kids do. "You did this!" "Well you did this before!" "Unnn unnn, no I didn't!" "Yes, you did!" "Well mine is bigger than yours!" So on and so forth.

It's hard to not be selfish in any relationship. We want things to go our way in life in general, so when this person stands up to us and tells us how our actions are affecting them and that we should stop, how dare they stop me from doing something I either like to do or apparently didn't think was wrong. How dare I stop yelling at you. I've been yelling at people all my life. How dare you tell me to stop expecting you to be perfect and do everything I say. Wasn't that why I got married in the first place?

Well, yes it was. You did get married thinking this person was supposed to fulfill every need everyone else missed or messed up in life plus the ones they got right. He or she was supposed to be superman or superwoman. The scenes we grew up on from our favorite family television shows, the things we enjoyed around our own homes, and the things we often imagined in our heads. All of these grandiose things we want in our own marriages all while failing to see how we contribute to the demise of it all.

When we fail to see ourselves, we fail to improve ourselves. Your marriage isn't perfect, so what are you going to do about it? Just because the clique says it is not perfect doesn't make it a lost case or worth not trying to get better.

Self-improvement is the key. Realizing the need to improve is the first step. And let me say this. Self-improvement is forever needed. I thrive on it. But

144

what I had to realize while I was constantly improving my working level behavior with how I operated with my employees and with management was that I had to learn how to operate with my husband and kids, too.

I had to take time to explore self. I had to really think about what my husband was saying to me and get out of my feelings. Eventually, his negative perception of me became his view of me, and it did prove challenging, but I had to work on changing my narrative in his eyes. You see, just like I had a story and a side, so did he. I had to not only listen to him but understand his side. He was selfish, but so was I.

It's no wonder we've become selfish when you look at what and how most of us are doing in our marriages now as opposed to the past. Gone are the days of marriage at the tender age of 21. We are getting married later and later these days. Women and men are purchasing their first home independently and doing just fine. There was a time when such things needed the help of a spouse to maintain. Not anymore. So, we are living our own lives with our own rules. No parents to dictate our goings and comings. No one making us go to bed at a certain time or waking us up. We make up our own rules as we go, oftentimes adopting many of the rules we were raised on.

Then here comes another person who had the same amount of time to do the same things as you. "I.N.D.E.P.E.N.D.E.N.T. What do you know about me?" (For those around my age, that was a popular rap song.) We are now so darn independent and set in our ways, that it is starting to affect how we cohabitate with one another. And that, my friend, is the bottom line.

Do me a favor. Start listening to your spouse's top complaint. How often have they expressed how your independence is negatively affecting your marriage? It won't be in those words, but this is basically what it boils down to. Think deeply for a moment. Have you heard this before? Maybe from a boss, old girlfriend/boyfriend, best friend, or even from a parent? Be honest for a moment. Are you in fact guilty of doing this? I'll wait.

Are you guilty?

If so, why is it that you continue this behavior? Too hard to change? You've been this way all your life, so it must just be the way that you are? Bull crap!

You can change! Want to stop being an asshole in your marriage? Easy! Stop being an asshole in your marriage! You're an asshole on your job! Asshole at the grocery store. Your spouse didn't just make that up. You've been an asshole all your life! So what, your mama or daddy were assholes, and you learned assholing from them. That does NOT give you permission to die an asshole.

You CAN change! Repeat after me, "I can change." Don't just say it in your head, say it out loud. Speak into the atmosphere, "I can change!" It's not that hard. Well, it is hard, sort of. But it can be done, if you want to do it. It will take time. Let's be real, you've been this way for some time. Bishop Jakes refers to this as your 'default settings.'

For example, computers typically come already set-up to do certain functions. If those settings work for you, you allow them to remain, and that is what you operate with (Times New Roman font, size 12). If someone else uses your computer and changes the settings, don't you automatically notice it? And what is it that we do? We tell ourselves that something is different and that we don't like it. Once we notice what happened, we change it back to our preferred setting, our *default* setting.

Your attitude and how you treat others has become your go-to default settings. It is what is normal for you and what you are used to. It's your comfort zone. And we all can contest to the fact that it is hard changing those things that we are comfortable with. Once we change or try to change, it looks funny at first. It doesn't feel right anymore, and we don't like it. We like the old self. Why change who we are?

Well, it's simple. Who we are or who we are used to being is hurting someone else. Period. Just that simple. What you are doing is hurting someone you say you love with all of your heart. You vowed to be with this person through thick and thin, yet you won't sacrifice self for them. How can we confess to everyone and the Lord to be with someone through sickness and health all while causing pain and stress that we refuse to modify? Stress kills. Oftentimes, we are the culprit. We are the ones causing the most pain to those we say we love, and we often refuse to change for them. How much do you really love them? Love them enough to change?

For the sake of my marriage, we had to change. That means I had to change. I had to realize the pressures I was evoking on my husband through my long scroll of expectations. All the things I thought a husband ought to be doing for his wife, doing around the house, and in front of those who viewed us. I treated him like he had more to give than me. I acted as if everything rested on his shoulders, and I constantly reminded him of things as if I were his mother. I was out of order, but if I wanted to love this man unconditionally, I had to give that same gracious love.

It wasn't about Nakia anymore. It was about James and Nakia as one. My independence taught me a lot on how to handle myself in this cruel world, but it taught me little on how to conduct myself in my marriage with another human being with feelings just like I had. I encourage you that if you can relate to being like me in any of this, please take some time to evaluate yourself. We always find it far easy to know what he needs to do all while ignoring anything that us women should be doing. Take stock of self and be as real as you can about who you are and how you act in your marriage. No need in being fake with yourself thinking you are all that, right all the time, and nothing about you needs to change. If you feel that way, I wish you all the best. I dare not criticize you. Life sometimes is the best teacher.

12
Getting Over the Hurt

Once you have crossed the desert of selfishness, one has to look back over the sands at what has been passed through with fresh eyes. Not of eyes of damnation or of disdain, but eyes of forgiveness and trust. This proved to be the most daunting task in our marriage, and it will be just as challenging for you. It will be the hardest thing you will ever be asked to do. Ever.

Not everyone has my story. You have your own. Mine doesn't trump yours and vice versa. Along the way, we all have been challenged tremendously within our own walls of safety, and it hurt us really, really bad. We've lost sleep over the years in our marriages, and we've cried many tears. Many cave experiences. Yet, it still remains. Forgiving our spouses and/or learning to trust them repeatedly is mandatory. And that, too, will be the hardest thing we'll ever do.

The heart is fragile and oh so sensitive. I don't believe anyone can hurt us the way a spouse can. That is why it's so damaging and hard to put things they do behind us. When we marry, our hearts are exposed, so when they hurt us, we are scarred for life. But that doesn't have to be your story. It's not mine.

After counseling, I knew the road to trusting James again would be hard. I had his passwords, but with all the passwords in the world, nothing could shake the feeling of him not deserving my trust. It is not that he didn't deserve it. He had to *earn it back*. I'd sort of erased the trust I had for him, and somehow, it had to be rewritten back into our marriage. This would take some time for sure

Actually, I had to will the courage into existence. I had to tell myself over and over again that I would trust my husband. He did help me with this by making sure he didn't give me any kind of reason to question his behavior. The thing that was hard about this was that, overall, he seemed to have respected our marriage—from what I could see. He came in at a respectable time. He never went missing or was unreachable. If I asked him anything, I received a prompt response. I mean he was good at sneaking around without me noticing. I never really wondered about him.

Now that I had a reason to worry, it took a lot of mental strength to control my wandering thoughts. Fighting with my husband due to constant speculations wasn't on my agenda before or after the infidelity. I just didn't want to do it. It wasn't who I was. I've said it plenty throughout this book. I was not that girl. Nor did I want to turn into her.

I've always been confident in who I was and was confident in my relationship. There was no need to change that now. I may have suffered a whipping, but I wasn't beat down by far. Doesn't matter how any woman looked that he conversed with, I was still me. I'm not a bad catch. I am a good one matter-of-fact. So regardless of what he did, I wasn't going to lose me.

Occasionally, I'd slip though. Something would trigger the thought of what he did, and I would just snap and say something vicious out of the blue. Without knowing what happened, he would go into defense, and I would chew him up and spit him out with my words. Just like that, we wouldn't be talking for a few days.

I hated I was doing this, and I knew it wasn't helping us none. It was making things worse. I forgave him. I did. There was no way we were together if I hadn't forgiven him. The issue now was that I hadn't forgotten. I still remembered, and it still hurt. When those triggers would happen, it felt like I was reading those emails all over again for the first time.

Sometimes the reminders would drive me to read them if I was at work. So why not just delete them? I couldn't. I just couldn't. There were a few times I'd read them and became furious all over again. At least one of those random times, it drove me to email James a nasty message, and there we were again. Fighting and hurting each other.

There were times he'd wanted to give up. I can recall him saying, "You aren't going to ever truly forgive me. We will never get past this." I mean I wanted to get past it really, really bad, but it was so darn hard. Once those thoughts were back into my brain, I just couldn't get past it. But I knew exactly what he was saying. We weren't healthy anymore. We were becoming toxic.

Even though I agreed with him, I just

couldn't come to realization of the situation. So, I'd yell out in frustration, "You don't understand! But fuck it! I won't say nothing else. No worries. I asked one thing, and it led to me being insecure. Well fuck it and fuck you. You won't have me insecure over your ass no more. I won't be asking you another thing."

Maybe not the first time did I screamed such things and it became true. But about the third time, it did. Even if my mind was over in the gutter, I willed my mouth shut. I wouldn't give in to the temptation of starting a fight. Eventually, it worked. I will say it took about a year and a half later before I think 'forgetting' had started taking place.

Forgetting does not mean your mind will never recall the situation. Doesn't mean you will never receive a reminder, but what it does mean is that when those thoughts enter your mind, there will not be any feelings attached. Think about it. I forgave James, but when the reminder surfaced, I would get angry all over again as if it just happened. Yes, I forgave him to restore our marriage, but I hadn't forgotten.

When I could see that folder with those messages and face them without frowning, that is when I knew I was stronger. When I wasn't tempted to read them, I was even stronger. And when I could talk to him after those thoughts, I knew I was a beast. But it took a while for me, so please have patience with yourself. The most important thing is being true to your feelings. Your feelings are real. They aren't to feel ashamed about, and he or she shouldn't push you to believe they aren't real. They are real. And they can hurt for a while.

It took me a year and a half, but I'm not the standard, I'm just an example. Everyone is different. The advice that I gave myself is to keep trying at it. Don't give up. It is possible to forgive again and to forget forever and start back trusting your spouse.

I have to be honest. I know you are wondering what I did with access to all of his emails and social media accounts. I checked them hoes! That's what I did. No reason in lying.

Within that period of working on forgetting everything, whenever crazy thoughts would come to my head, I'd start immediately stalking his emails and Facebook. I would be all up and through there. Yes, I was.

I'd be re-reading messages I had already

read looking for stuff. Listen, a woman scorned can become a lunatic real quick. You know how you can have notifications to come to you when your Facebook has been opened from another unknown or unfamiliar computer, right? Well he had that setting enabled. But let me tell you what I was doing. I'd open his Facebook and then go to another browser and open up his email and delete the notification. Go into the trash bin and delete it from there. I mean I was a sneaky somebody.

Crazy thing is, I couldn't help it. At the beginning, I had become obsessed with checking his messages and Facebook. I'm not sure if he knew this or not. Well now he knows. But just like I got better, I got better at eliminating this craziness, too.

Years later, I can honestly say I can't remember the last time I've gone into my husband's emails or Facebook accounts. I don't even know the passwords, I don't think. I have no desire to look. I've been delivered. I love and trust my man. But one thing is for sure, he knows his wife is crazy. Wink.

13
His Promise

This isn't a self-help book by far, so I don't have a 12-step plan to foolproof your marriage. I only have my experience and who we are as a result of it. I'm not idolizing it. It hurt like hell at the time. But it is over with and done. I can't change the past, only the future, and our future is bright like the diamonds.

I don't know if this happens to everyone, but when I see Facebook friends, associates, and what have you out and about, they often tell me how they love my family. The enjoy reading my posts about my family and think I have a beautiful marriage. I just thank them, but sometimes I wonder if they know my story. Well they do now, and I'm unashamed of it.

This is my testimony. This is my story. Along this journey of helping married couples, God spoke to me and said that if I was going to help them I had to "tell it." I kept hearing the words *tell it*. Of course, I was afraid. First of all, my husband would curse me out if he thought I was going to tell all *his* business like this. I'm still scare at what he thinks about this book. He is probably just letting me have my way. Or better yet, he is probably helping me follow the Master's plans.

The morning I wrote these very lines, someone sent me Jeremiah 29:11: "For I know the plans I have for YOU, declares the LORD. Plans to prosper you and not harm you, plans to give you hope and a future." As I read the preview of that message, I started crying out. You see the night before, I'd become extremely afraid of what my husband would think once he read this manuscript. I started thinking about his reactions, realizing I didn't think he was expecting me to *tell it*, tell it.

But if you are reading this, that means he has blessed its release, and I am thankful the enemy didn't prevent us from using our serum to heal someone's marriage. During my own, I can't say I had anything tangible to assist me. I was learning off the seat of my pants. The counseling was good, but unless I was going each year, it would soon fade away, and we would be left to figure it out on our own.

We were determined. Just like him, I wanted my family, so I was willing to put down pride of being cheated on. The embarrassment wasn't worth my son growing up with his father not living with him. I didn't just do it for my son. I did it for me, too, because you see, I did still love him. The damage was done, but it didn't erase the love.

It didn't erase God's promise either. A year or so later, I was with another child, and James and I were searching for a church home...together...as a family. Praise God! We spent that whole year of my pregnancy looking for a church with our name on it. I asked James to pray about the right church for us while I was praying for James. I didn't want to make the decision, nor did I want to rush it. We visited this one church for a few months, but it wasn't working for us. It was a large, known church, so we by nature were trying to make it fit. Through prayer, I mentioned to James that we didn't have to stay, that we could keep looking.

So we did. I can remember this billboard down the street from our house. He mentioned that we could try that church out one day. Said he went to school with that pastor. That spelled out to me that the guy was young. I remember telling him, "I don't want to go *play* church." How wrong was I?

We visited that church on a whim one Sunday. Everyone was so welcoming and nice. I'm not a hugger, well a little bit of a hugger, but they gave them out so freely, and they felt sincere. After listening to this young pastor preach, at one point, James and I looked over at each like whoa. This guy was on fire for the Lord, and he had an old soul. He was whooping and everything. If you've ever been to a Southern Baptist church, you should know what whooping is. And it didn't bother me, but I was afraid that from my husband's conservative church background, the whooping would turn him off. But it didn't.

It was in November when we started visiting Pine Grove, and then we missed a couple Sundays due to Christmas travel to my hometown. Once we arrived homed, with the hood of the car still warm, James received a phone call. It was the pastor. He was checking on us because we hadn't been to church in a couple of weeks. James hung up the phone in shock.

It meant a lot to him that we were missed.

We had us a new home. And have been there ever since.

Promise = Fulfilled

EPILOGUE

Writing a memoir of a tragic event can scare you because although you're not telling *all* your secrets, it does expose you to the world. But someone recently blessed me when I told her about my concerns after writing the book. She said, "Once the veil is pulled back, the enemy can't attack you there anymore. He has to work a little harder to think of something else because that right there won't work."

Telling my story was therapeutic as it allowed me to bring forth those past memories and deal with them from my current position. So much has happened over the years, but one thing that has changed is who is fighting whom. James and I are a team now. We fight together. One thing I joke about with people is that I can count on my hand how often James and I have fought over the years since *the* event. I'm not saying we don't fight now, but there is no comparison. Then, it occurred nearly every week; now, it might be quarterly, and when it happens, we *communicate*.

Another thing I can note is that James and I are stronger than we've ever been. This attribute continues to strengthen with the passing of days, months, and years. We are more confident with one another. My confidence arises when I'm able to allow him quiet time, or cave experiences, without bothering him nor wrongly assuming his issue is automatically my issue or that it is because of me. I no longer constantly question his love for me. One thing I know is that Mr. Redmon loves his wife.

My husband is still quiet about his feelings so I really don't know how or if this writing helps him. It is very possible he allowed this to simple shut me up by giving me my way. I wouldn't say I'm spoiled or anything but James does take pride in giving me what I ask for, within reason. I'm sure he is thrilled to really know where I stand with those past issues. Meaning that I am truly over them and not holding his indiscretions over him for life. He knows I have forgiven and forgotten this and that I have moved on with our love. He knows our bond is unbreakable.

Agreeing to marry James was the easy part, but it is a fight to stay married to him. So many things in this world can bring a marriage down. Temptations are always lurking around the corners awaiting to trip us up. It's a fight to stay in this thing. And the fighting will never cease. The worst mistake you will ever make in your marriage is to let your guard down.

Wherefore they are no more twain, but one flesh. What therefore God hath joined together, let no man put asunder (Matthew 19:6 KJV).

ABOUT THE AUTHOR

Dr. Redmon is a financial manager for the United States Army. She spends her spare time motivating everyone in her path, either through one-on-one interactions or mentoring, public speaking, her blog, or simply by walking her walk. Through prayer, reflection, and listening, Dr. Redmon discovered her life's purpose. Therefore, her goal is to inspire, if but one person, to find their purpose in life and to live it…unapologetically. Even though she can be the most optimistic, cup staying on full person you'd ever meet, know this: she is willing to go toe-to-toe over her man, Mr. James H. Redmon, Jr. But no misunderstandings, this is a tag-team effort when it comes to their union (wink). When they are not gazing into each other's eyes, whispering sweet nothings in each other's ears (yeah right), James and Nakia are spending their time repeating poetry like "put that down," "leave your sister alone," "no he didn't, I saw you the whole time," "stop running in my house," and other sweet sayings to their two beautiful children, James III (Trey) and London.

You can learn more about Dr. Redmon on her blog, Competition of 1: https://competitionof1.com/.